The Black Equinox
Rise of Agbaka

DANIEL A EPIH

Copyright © 2023 by. Daniel A Epih All rights reserved.

No part of this book may be reproduced in any form or by any electronic or mechanical means, including information storage and retrieval systems, without written permission from the author, except for the use of brief quotations in a book review.

Published by: Book Writing Founders
www.bookwritingfounders.co.uk

Introduction

There is a time in everyone's life when we get carried away by our own self belief in how strong we are or about how strong our position is well defended and fortified. This is even more so if we perceive our rival or opponent as weak and easy to handle or defeat. Unfortunately, there are always things we do not and will never truly know about others because that is just the way life works.

The Obare people have conquered every tribe and country around them apart from this small group of people on a small piece of land. Yet, they are very prosperous and that makes conquering them desirable in every way.

There is motivation and drive, by all means for this land to be taken, but no one has ever dared to attack them.

History had little to offer as to why they have been left untouched and so this is the dilemma that the Dauntless Emperor faced, made worse by the fact that every one of his senior officers and his most trusted high priest, though scared of him as they should, still summoned the courage to tell him he should stay away from Uzi.

Stubbornness, pride and greed can sometimes blight our sense of good judgement, but at what cost?

Dedication

This book is dedicated to Mrs. Margaret Epih, Rev. Eddy Omoruyi Okundaye and Audrone Jurkenaite.

I would like to thank the following people for their support, Mrs R Ross, Mags Robertson, Denise Cripps and Mary Epih. You all encouraged me on this project when I needed it the most.

Catherine Amboa, thanks for believing in this dream and being part of the journey! Blessed to be working with you.

Contents

Introduction	*iv*
Dedication	*v*
Appreciation	*vii*
An Empire Mourns	*1*
Igue, The Festival Of Kings	*6*
Counsel	*11*
The Oorun Keep	*16*
The Hall Of Fallen Kings	*21*
The Price Of Peace	*25*
Violence	*31*
Romance	*35*
Bloodshed And Burning	*40*
The Third Son	*43*
Enogie, High Priestess Of The Moon	*49*
Amira	*55*
Fury	*60*
The Black Equinox	*67*
The Pig Paddock	*71*
Fearlessness And Failure	*74*
Damage	*78*

Appreciation

When I was 5 years old, I wanted to start primary school with the other children a year early. After enduring days of me crying every morning, my mum decided to register me at school. I finished primary school and passed my entrance exam to grammar school. We could not afford to pay the fees and all the other expenses. So, Mum asked me what I wanted to do. I told her that if we could not afford the fees, I could learn how to fix cars. She took me to the garage to register me as an apprentice and they asked for a registration fee as high as the school fees. So, she decided she would rather pay the school fees. We went back home and she took some of her jewellery and clothes, sold them, paid my fees and I started school.

Six years later, I got my grades and was offered admission into two universities. One was to study Mathematics and the other Business Administration and Management. If I chose to study Maths at the federal university, it would be cheaper as I would pay almost nothing. I knew though that that was not my calling and told Mum I would rather study Business Administration and Management. I can still see the tears running down her face as she explained to me, 'But you know, we cannot afford it'.

There were no student loans to cover the costs of tuition, accommodation and books for the four years at university. She looked at me and assured me that God would do it and I graduated from university four years later.

I would not be here today if it were not for my Mum's courage and support.

A heartfelt 'thank you' to all the parents out there who make dreams come true!

An Empire Mourns

All the mewling was beginning to grate on Agbaka. None of these people really knew his father – and if he could hold it together, they all should. He wondered if he could outlaw crying.

Imaghodo, the palace's most fawning seer, droned on:

'... at the hands of traitors. We can only thank the ancestors that they failed in the fullness of their evil scheme. That Agbaka the Dauntless, the Emperor's third son, survives, ensures the great house of Obare marches forth, continuing to lead us towards our sun-drenched future. Long live the Gleaming Emperor!'

Cheers echoed around the barren white walls of the Throne Temple, the spacious reverberations only amplifying their hollowness. Their empty praise was of no consequence. They needn't love him, they need only know what he was capable of. And they did. This was a period of mourning and every male in Obare must shave their head as a sign of respect to the late king. Agbaka refused to have his head shaven and who could question the new king?

The imperial throne was carved from solid sandstone: a stupid material to make a chair out of, Agbaka thought, and his backside agreed. With a mind to distract himself from the incessant whimpering, he cast his gaze to the mosaic ceiling. Coloured stones from every region of the Laruba Expanse, spiralling out in the shape of a vast, dazzling sun, a symbol of Obare's reach. It stood for more than that now, for trade was no longer the only hold Agbaka's empire had on the four corners of the subcontinent. With Agbaka at his side, his father had overseen the greatest territorial expansion of any ruler in history. From the eastern Untameable Grasslands to the western Abe-okuta Rainforest and the impassable Karajaan Desert to the north, almost anywhere that could be conquered, had been. The rest had bent the knee to the throne at Obare for centuries. The rainbow colours of the stones, mortared into their respective places, twinkled in the dawn light.

Agbaka chuckled to himself as he realised that the mosaic was mirrored on the floor with its human counterpart: representatives from each of the Laruba Expanse's minor city - states, nations and people. He watched as they came forward, bowing dutifully and offering gifts to the immense imperial sarcophagus – as large as it was to allow space for the 12 sacrificed slaves (known optimistically as 'servants for the afterlife'). Their bony, malnourished corpses hardly made a comfortable bed for his father, he imagined.

First came Obare's city-states. Their loyalty was unquestioned, so Agbaka forgave the modest, albeit supplicant, offerings of perfumes and incense. Then it was on to foreigners, with the Kingdom of Zufani, Obare's oldest ally, at the front. How proud they were, in their long green gowns and false crowns. He wondered where that pride came from, given that they'd been nothing more than extensions of Obare since long before his father. An ancient familial connection had granted them the titles of 'King' and 'Queen', although they fooled no one but themselves. Their gift was a statue of his father. Great, thought Agbaka, just what this palace needed: more sandstone.

Then came the man from Ijaw, the vast swathe of swamps and mud-lands at the heart of the Laruba Expanse. He'd clearly had a wash. He had brought a pair of hippo and crocodile hides, and Agbaka imagined how many mudders had lost their lives for those. Following were the representatives of Obare's most recent conquest, the Ibutho Confederation, a barely organised collection of tamed warlords that oversaw vast legions of spear-wielding peasants. Numbers were no advantage against the Obare Lancers. They stooped before him in their leather skirts and brought forth two mighty war drums, made from at least three zebra hides. He actually quite liked those; Agbaka's recent 'visit' to the Southern Plains had clearly left him and his militarism well understood. Then came people from each of the edges of the territory, those that saw their tribes' survival in trade with the Empire. A desert man from the north brought a prize camel which shat, unceremoniously, at the base of the Zufani statue as it was pulled from the crowd. Agbaka stifled a cackle. The grass nomad from the east approached; he was so heavily draped in beads, Agbaka assumed they were the cause of his crooked spine. His offering was a pair of spears carved from giant rhino ivory. Agbaka imagined he'd be able to snap them over his knee and it wouldn't leave a bruise. Decorative weapons were an innovation he despised. The scarred man from the Abe-okuta Rainforest was next. Self-inflicted ridges covered his body in intricate patterns. Agbaka had always rather admired the custom; he thought it could be a good one to force on his feebler soldiers as a training exercise. The man did not break eye contact with Agbaka as he placed a fearsome war mask, as well-carved as his face, on the flagstones before him. He stepped back to leave the floor open.

The last in attendance to this sombre gift-giving were the representatives from Uzi, a strangely quiet and small nation of the Southern Expanse, just on the other side of the rainforest. Agbaka knew little of their people and their past; their staunch pacifism dissuaded him from any interest. History was forged in battle. There was nothing he could learn from them. The gift was borne by two women. They were the only people to have sent elders of the softer sex – the only people who had elders of the softer sex. Dressed in brightly coloured silks and well-laden with jewels, they carried two wooden chests. The first woman peeled back the intricate golden clasp and heaved open the box to reveal a bounty of fruits Agbaka had never seen before. He could not imagine how they'd lasted at the peak of their ripeness all the way from Uzi. Then the second woman presented her chest, and Agbaka blinked as its contents sparkled, flinging sunlight into his eyes. They were jewels fit for an emperor, undoubtedly worth more than the rest of the contributions combined. Agbaka made sure that the impression this Uzian gift had left on him did not show.

Suddenly, consumed with questions about Uzi, the rest of the funeral washed over Agbaka. It was well known that they had never been conquered by any of the empires of the past. He couldn't even remember a time when someone had tried; his father certainly hadn't. Why? What stopped Obare from reaching out and taking this jewel of the Laruba Expanse? Clearly, the years of stability and peace had been kind to these people of the valley; they had amassed wealth and technology unrivalled by even his own. He felt a familiar feeling, the one he let flow in battle. But there was no Ibutho shield-wielder to cut down here. It made him restless.

As the people filtered out at the end of proceedings, Agbaka did not wait around. He dashed to Imaghodo, who was gently ushering people out of the Throne Temple. He grabbed him by the arm, pulled him to the pile of gifts and pointed to the Uzian chests.

'Why do we allow such wealth outside of our Empire, Imaghodo?'

'Lustrous Emperor, the people of Uzi are valuable trading partners and good friends of your father. Their prosperity benefits all the nations of this great land.' This simpering sycophant was avoiding his question. He pushed harder.

'Theirs is the richest and most fertile territory in the Expanse. Why have we not taken it for ourselves?'

'You should not trouble yourself with questions of war on this day of mourning, Dauntless One.'

Agbaka pushed Imaghodo back, sending him stumbling over the mask. The seer fell against the sarcophagus and looked up, trembling.

'Do not tell me what I should and should not trouble myself with. Why did we never invade Uzi?' Imaghodo, never one for confrontation, whimpered.

'I apologise, Gleaming Emperor, I do not know.' 'Then what use are you, seer? Who does know?'

The fool dropped his eyes to the floor, nervous of the answer he was about to give.

'Your Dauntlessness... no one does.'

Young men shaving their head as they mourn the late king

Igue, The Festival Of Kings

It was as though all the colour, noise and exuberance of the festival's spectacle faded into nothing. Did she know he was looking at her? He thought he probably wanted her to know, but then what? Her eyes darted up and met with his and it was as though a wildebeest stampede cascaded across his chest. He looked away. He knew she had seen him, clear as the moon, but he pretended he'd been watching the acrobats all along. He was certain that he was unconvincing.

He normally loved Igue. It was, ordinarily, his favourite day of the year. As a child, he'd leap about pretending to be one of the horse runners, landing backflips off the back of a charging zebra, the crowd chanting his name. He loved the singing and dancing too... but the singers and dancers themselves? This year, clearly, was different. All the fireworks in Uzi couldn't light up the valley like Khanyishiwa. Cheers erupted from the masses, seemingly amplified by the roar of Inyanga Waterfall crashing down behind the stage. Xola didn't notice.

'OUCH!' He felt a stabbing jab in his ribs. His mother's elbows seemed to sharpen the older he got.

'Xola,' she muttered.

'What!?' he replied, feigning ignorance.

'You are positively drooling. Show some respect for those performers.'

'I don't know what you're talking about,' he said with a smirk.

'Be a king, not a boy.'

But I'm both, he thought.

He supposed his mother was right; she always was. And this wasn't 'Igue, the Festival of *Boys*' after all. Although, it didn't really seem to be about kings either. For all the staged reverence of ancestors and royalty past, no one ever talked about who they were or what they did. It was sunset worship, showing off and gift-giving; no one thought twice about it. There was value, no doubt, in his people celebrating themselves. And inviting foreigners to join in their joy was worthwhile too. The walls of their valley sheltered the Uzian people from the terrifying wilderness of the world above; their city and the vast delta it overlooked was an enduring oasis of peace and prosperity. Xola looked to the top of Inyanga Waterfall and wondered if those plains might be safer if more people saw the festivities at Igue. Khanyishiwa's dancing would be a balm for anyone's suffering.

He relaxed as she and her troupe took to the stage. For a moment, his responsibilities as boy and king were as one. The drummers burst into life: fractal rhythms providing a pillar for the dancers to gyrate around. Maybe he was too smitten, but Xola was sure that the rattles on Khanyishiwa's ankles crackled with greater precision than anyone else's. In his eyes, she was the most beautiful cultural dancer in the whole of Uzi. One thing he did know of the past was that these expressions of talent and showmanship were the legacy of a tradition that used to have higher stakes. The Igue festival of his day is unbelievably different from what his ancestors witnessed. Back then, the festival was all about power, it was the opportunity for all those with special powers from all over the land to come and display their powers before the king. If anyone's sorcery was deemed greater than that of the ruler, they would be banished. Xola felt it a shame, of course, that wielders of such mystical power were consigned to an ailing collective memory but was grateful that he no longer had to banish those more powerful than himself. Khanyishiwa would be consigned to the Abe-okuta Rainforest in an instant.

Bright flashes of exploding colour indicated to the revellers that the performances had end. Fireworks were a way for Uzi to evoke the power of the Azen without the fear they were said to induce. Yelps from the city suggested that Uzi's dogs had not learned the difference. With the sun long gone, drinking and eating were the order of the evening, and Xola's role became more active. It was a time when the king and his people ate as one family; socialising was paramount. Fortunately, Xola had never struggled to make conversation, no matter how dull some of his more aged subjects could be. It also meant he could speak to Khanyishiwa.

Xola grabbed and loaded up a bowl of roasted warthog from the man at the spit and kept an eye out for his romantic flame's glow. He bluffed his way through a conversation about the latest innovations in irrigation technology, feigned interest for the fireworks master who insisted on telling him how they'd 'achieved purple' and was sincerely impressed with a jewellery designer pitching for a royal model. Unfortunately, none of it held his attention for as long as would have been polite; on each occasion, Khanyishiwa taunted him by passing through his field of vision. She knew what she was doing, surely. By the time he'd agreed to wear an uzanite-encrusted rose-gold arm cuff, he'd given up on playing coy. He hurriedly told Gugu he'd show it to his mother and darted off in Khanyishiwa's direction.

There she was, bathed in moonlight by the Inyanga plunge pool. Her eyes met his as he approached. That stampede made its way down his spine, but his composure held this time.

Just as he thought of his opening line… he felt a tap on his shoulder and someone spoke. The accent was strange and foreign:

'King Xola?' Possibly northern, but it was rare to have people from those parts here. They were hardened mountain types known to feel claustrophobic in this sheltered and humid air. He turned to find himself faced with a pair of men, tall and gaunt in stature, their faces taut and wind-battered: definitely northerners.

'Welcome to Uzi, dear friends! Such a pleasure to host you on this most auspicious of evenings. Have you enjoyed the festivities?' This was the first time he'd used that line and it hadn't been met with a smile. It was only then he noticed their clothes: they were draped in the bright colours and sparkling jewellery favoured by his own people and none of the stark whites and earth tones he'd come to expect from mountain folk. The man that spoke hesitated, realising his efforts to blend in had failed. The second showed no such lapse.

'Without question, your highness,' he said, calmly. 'Please, call me Xola!'

'You preside over such riches, Xola, both of the earth and otherwise. We are honoured to have borne witness to the beauty of the Uzian people.'

'It is not over yet, esteemed friends!' he said, indicating to the bubbling crowd behind him. 'But you must please excuse me, I'm running late,' he said, doing his best to appear cordial whilst taking his leave. But the strange wolf in sheep's clothing was persistent.

'Your forefathers must have won countless great battles to ensure such wealth. We can only imagine their might.'

Xola was losing patience now. 'I'm afraid you are mistaken, sir. The walls of Uzi Valley and the mighty ocean beyond are all that protect us. It is our peace that begets prosperity.' It was another set of well-rehearsed lines, but the man was unconvinced. A strange silence befell them. Xola remembered Khanyishiwa. 'Igue Vuya,' he insisted, forcing a smile and making for the water's edge.

By the time he'd cleared the crowd, Khanyishiwa had gone. Not that it mattered at that point. These strange interlopers had all but killed his sense of romance.

Igue Festival

Counsel

The reports had repeated on him like undercooked meat. Supposedly, just on the other side of the Abe-okuta, the land's fatted pig wallowed, stupid and defenceless. Ordinarily, his mouth would be watering at the prospect, but something stayed his appetite. Unused to being unsure, and guarded about this novel bout of anxiety, Agbaka had summoned Obare's war council to their first meeting since the annexation of the Ibutho's Southern Plains. It was also the first time he'd sat at the head of its table.

This chair was considerably more luxurious than the throne. It made sense, he thought: Obare's emperors tended to be at their most comfortable conquering. The table was shaped like an arrow tip, a steep and sharp triangle. He sat alone on its shortest side, the equal, longer sides to his left and right coming to a tip directly in front of him, pointing to a cavernous archway that framed a view of the Laruba Expanse. From their vantage point in the Taraba Mountains, it was as though the rest of the land tumbled away from them. At that moment, it occurred to Agbaka that this table's arrow may point directly at Uzi, just out of sight beyond the rainforest, and this particular meeting may be making good on the table's long-destined purpose. He did away with the thought quickly; whatever was causing his uncharacteristic hesitation would not be solved with superstition.

'Enough, Imaghodo. I'm in no mood for your droning,' he said, aware his uncertainty wouldn't be resolved by pomp and oratory either. Imaghogo quivered as he obliged, taking his seat to Agbaka's left. 'Tell the council what you told me, Karimu.'

Karimu, Chief of Imperial Intelligence, stood stiffly. 'The intelligence from our instruments in Uzi is definitive. The city, while drenched in wealth, technology and culture, has no standing army and no defensive capabilities to speak of.' Karimu almost looked reluctant. He watched as disquiet settled among those present, their Emperor's intentions now apparent. Agbaka considered dismissing them there and then. *What use was a war council made nervous by war?*

'"The walls of Uzi Valley and the mighty ocean beyond are all that protect us,"' Agbaka said, doing his best southern accent. He waited for a reaction, but none came. '"Our peace begets prosperity," so they say.' Again, nothing. 'Does any one of you have a thought to share? Uzi's wealth has gone unchecked for too long. Unchallenged, they could amass power and strength to destabilise the entire Obare Empire. It sits unguarded and unaware.' The silence lingered a little longer. Agbaka let it. 'What is your counsel?' he demanded finally.

'Gleaming Emperor!' It was the Zufani prince who first found the confidence to speak. Arrogance, in his case. 'I do not doubt your ability to bring this nation to heel. But, I am not convinced they are the threat you describe. If they had plans to expand or destabilise anybody, do you not think we would have felt it by now? They are a hermit kingdom, tucked away at the base of a waterfall, too busy singing and dancing to worry about the world atop the walls of their valley.'

'Such strange faith you have in these foreigners, foreigner,' Agbaka quipped. 'Even the lion, lord of the forest, protects himself against flies.' The prince's lips tightened and remained shut.

'Anyone else?' Agbaka asked. 'I don't remember my father's meetings being so quiet. What about you, Soasoro?' He turned to the man closest to his right, his First Blade, commander of the Imperial Army. His wrinkled face twitched, seemingly surprised to be called upon.

'Forgive me, Dauntless One. I am no diplomat. I do not claim to understand the affairs of foreign nations or the concerns of statecraft. But I know that there are 30,000 of the best-trained men this world has ever seen sat ready to answer the call of those that do.'

'A rather wordy way of saying nothing at all, Soasoro. Why do you all hold your tongues?' No one seemed to be able to hold his gaze. It was rare, but sometimes, the fear Agbaka instilled in those around him was counterproductive. 'Honestly, I share your trepidation. I want to invade Uzi, but if it was as easy as it looked, someone would have done it by now. Give me open and honest counsel – or I shall have to find new counsel.'

It was Karimu who spoke first. 'The apprehension you speak of has precedent, Emperor. There are folkloric tales, mostly emanating from the Abe-okuta, that tell of great misfortune for anyone who seeks power in Uzi Valley. The peace they keep is said to be sacred and anyone who breaks it will themselves be broken. It was a warning heeded by many of your forefathers, the late Emperor Asaba among them.'

The knot in his stomach churned and Agbaka felt a wave of nausea wash over him. He swallowed it and looked to the rest of the council: on his right, nothing but hardened warlords – and not a word of disagreement from any of them.

'You all believe this too? Arruan?' he said to his First Spear, leader of the Obare Lancers.

'I don't know what to believe, Imperius. The river that leaves the Taraba mountains is pure. But by the time it crashes over the edge of Uzi Valley, it has passed through the Abe-okuta. Who knows what sorcery it has picked up along the way?' Arruan was the closest thing Agbaka had to a peer on the battlefield. It was a kinship he trusted over blood, but the answer was frustratingly vague.

'So no one knows anything? Has anyone considered that these legends may be a lie concocted by the cowards?'

'It would be a miraculous lie, Emperor, centuries in the making,' Karimu said.

Having sat quietly just to the left of the arrow's tip, Obaseki, Chief Arbiter and head of the Imperial War Chest finally spoke up. 'Forgive me if this is a poor question, Gleaming Emperor, but what do you really want from such an invasion? You cannot be seriously concerned for the security of the empire when one so dauntless sits on the throne.'

Obaseki was flying close to the sun. And he knew the answer to his poor question. But there were none more intelligent at this table than he, so Agbaka took the bait.

'For my father's legacy: the might of our empire. Uzi has wealth and technology that is wasted on them. These profligate pacifists must learn their place.'

Obaseki smiled. 'If it is their wealth and technology you want, you should ask for it. The Uzians have a non-negotiable commitment to peace. Threaten war and demand whatever you feel would be better used in Obare. They love gift-giving. Give them the opportunity to give the biggest in history.'

Agbaka asking Imaghodo if he should invade Uzi

The Oorun Keep

The birds looked different up here. They were bigger for one thing. And less plentiful.

Xola imagined that their more faded colours were a reflection of the landscape. The verdancy and vibrancy of Uzi Valley and the rainforest above meant no animal was out of place in greens, reds and yellows. Here, the birds were all the colours of sand and stone. An extended, rasping shriek rang out from above. He'd seen and heard so many great vultures in the three weeks since they passed Obesi, they no longer made him jump. He wondered if they'd been following the caravan or if there was just that much death around here.

Xola was grateful at least for the time spent with his horse. Asi had been faithful, loving and stoic throughout, and even now, at their road's steepest incline, she was nothing other than charming. He'd tried, once or twice, to convince some of the guards to race him. Sharp looks from his mother put an end to those notions before they'd even agreed on a finish line. She knew full well that he had no intention of joining her in the royal palanquin, but it didn't stop her from suggesting it three times a day. If he was going to leave the safety of Uzi Valley, he'd make sure he and Asi got a run around.

The road skirting the Abe-okuta had been flat and untroublesome, but most of the horses were unsettled by the forest's intimidating interior. He'd have felt the same if it wasn't for Asi's calm and untroubled presence. It got a little more interesting when the edge of the forest gave way to marshland. The diplomats' and traders' more experienced horses seemed to be able to sniff their way to solid ground, while he and Asi greatly enjoyed wallowing in the mud. The city of Obesi was challenging in its own way. The stone-paved streets and high walls left the whole place feeling claustrophobic. And the strange looks they'd gotten from the Obare faithful had not left them feeling welcome.

There was a sense of portent though as they crossed the Molili

River, a feeling that this journey was his first true challenge as king. And a challenge he could excel at. International diplomacy was not something Uzian rulers were used to, but winning people over was a natural talent of his. However, as the caravan made its way into the Taraba foothills, his self-assurance felt as stable as the sand, shale and rock that Asi was picking her way through. It was as though the ground here could fall from under you at any moment. By the time the fortress at Obare came into view, Xola was positively terrified.

The Molili River raged as it burst out from underneath the castle; its exit marking the only visible opening on an otherwise unbroken wall of brick. This formidable line of defence near perfectly sealed the gap between the mountain slopes on either side of the river's passage. The castle gates were, presumably, the only way to access the extensive plateau beyond this otherwise impassable mountain pass. The manmade walls were sheer and the same combination of beige, pink and grey found in the natural walls they seamlessly sat alongside.

Beyond and offset to the left was the Oorun Keep: a round box with sunburst ramparts and inner walls punctuated by triangular arches and pillars. Even nearing midday this immense fortress cast a shadow far enough down the valley to cloak Xola and his party for the rest of their journey. The wind howled as they wound their way up the final ascent. Xola shivered in the cold, dry air.

What awaited them behind those mighty gates was still something of an unknown. All the envoy had said was that 'the Emperor Agbaka' sought to 'negotiate' and that they should come without delay. His proposal had fallen on the twelfth moon and it was Uzian custom not to travel that month. His mother and advisors had all fretted about how Agbaka 'the Dauntless' might take a refusal, but Xola had insisted that tradition should trump diplomacy. In reality, he just wasn't ready to leave Khanyishiwa. He'd have refused the invitation outright had this man's character not been painted so viscerally. But now, in the shadow of this famously foul-tempered Emperor's fortress, Xola's head was spinning with gory possibilities. What did he want? Trade? Information? Perhaps it was optimism (and fear), but Xola was still hoping for friendship.

The road beneath them trembled as the mechanism behind the

gates' impressive locks clinked open. As if to startle them further, a horn somewhere in the keep blew so loudly that it frightened even the vultures off. Xola looked to his mother, who offered a calm nod.

'You should be the first to enter, my King,' she said.

He was no stranger to having to feign some posture or presence, but pretending not to be scared for your very life was a new experience.

Beyond the gates was a wide, winding staircase that brought them out by the parapet. He peered down the walls to the raging river below and it struck him that this violent water was the same water that meandered towards the ocean across the Uzi Delta. It was a long journey, a fact made all the more evident when he lifted his gaze and the snaking path of the Molili, guided his eye towards the horizon. Just over the far southern edge of the Abe-okuta sat his little kingdom. It had been true for some time, but it was an oppressive reality up here: he had never been so far from home. The rest of his company reached the top of the steps and gathered to await an escort.

After some time of silently being battered by the wind, they saw a man waddling down from the keep. That couldn't be Agbaka, could it? No. He was too short, too fat and too old. He arrived before them and caught his breath before introducing himself as 'the Palace's Premier Seer'. He was a doddery man who talked without concern for anyone listening. He seemed to be addressing the guards in the company and never once looked at Xola. Did he look so un-king-like? His heart sank. Through a wiry white beard, the seer mumbled something about 'great meetings of history' and his mother's 'fabled beauty failing to compare to reality' before asking them to follow him to the keep. The old man struggled up the steps, Xola's people politely slowing their walk to leave him in front.

They arrived in the Throne Temple, a spacious room of vaulted ceilings, high walls and open arches that allowed the cold wind to pass through uninterrupted. After insisting, the Emperor would receive them imminently, the seer took his seat to the left of the throne and sat, silently. The wait was long enough that he fell asleep, his snoring was the only thing to break the crippling silence.

'IMAGHODO!' The call came in an unforgiving tone. 'Fetch our guests some refreshments.' The man leapt to his feet without missing a beat and scuttled off to a room at the side. Xola looked up to where the voice had come from. There, standing to the side of the sandstone throne, was a man who could only have been Agbaka the Dauntless. Long, brown quilted fabric tied with golden thread hung from his immense and muscular frame. At his hip was a sheathed great sword with a stark, utilitarian hilt made of gold. His face was taut and sharp-edged with a jagged scar across his nose. *This was what kings were supposed to look like?*

Agbaka smiled, an expression Xola felt was more for him than the rest of his party. The Emperor's eyes scanned the Uzian envoy before resting on Xola.

'You must be the boy king.'

Boy king?

'Yes. Hello, I'm Xola. You must be the mighty Agbaka?'

'The mighty Emperor Agbaka. Yes. Welcome to Obare. You must forgive my seer. He is too old.'

'No, no, he was most cordial. In Uzi, we revere the aged; they offer so much wisdom.'

Agbaka laughed. 'The old are just those who didn't die when they should have. This world is for the young.'

'Then I'll count myself lucky!' Xola stole a glance at his mother, but her expression was unreadable. 'We are honoured to be in the presence of one so great, Emperor Agbaka. We must apologise for the delay to our travel. Our customs–'

'Your customs do not interest me,' Agbaka declared, cutting Xola off. 'I have invited you here with a view to sharing ours. Please. Come.' He descended the steps from the throne platform, and the party readied themselves to follow his lead. He turned and with a stony face said, 'No. Just the boy.'

Xola felt a wave of panic coursing through his body. Any sense of security that remained in him was drawn from the presence of his mother and their guard. His heart raced and his hands were clammier than when he first kissed Khanyishiwa. He turned to his mother. The panic in her eyes was well hidden. With near-perfect composure, she nodded him forward; he wished she hadn't. He wished she'd said 'Stay' or 'Not without a guard' or anything. But she didn't, so Xola turned back to his fellow king and followed.

Agbaka led Xola through to a small chamber to the side of the temple. It was dark, and a thick, ripe smell hung in the air. Taking a torch from the wall, Agbaka set it on a chandelier in the middle of the room. A ring of fire erupted from its touch and the room's grim decor revealed itself.

'This is the Hall of Fallen Kings. I'll leave it for you to make sense of the name,' he said with a wry smile. It wasn't much of a puzzle. Shrivelled heads, in varying degrees of age and decomposition, hung in a ring above the sun-shaped trough of fire, its flickering light giving these faces an otherworldly sense of animation. Upon each of the heads was a crown. The delicate silver ring that sat on Xola's head had never felt so uncomfortable.

The Hall Of Fallen Kings

Agbaka loved the smell in here. Sometimes he'd come just to be alone. This was the only place in the entire world where he felt any sense of connection to the ancestors his people spent so much time worshipping. Each of the heads in here was personally acquired by one of the emperors that came before him, trophies of each of their glorious conquests. The freshest trophy, the head of Yeye kaMpande, was the only one he'd watched fall from its body. He remembered the look in those eyes as Yeye had dropped to his knees. Agbaka was seconds away from decapitating the man himself, but something stayed his hand. He knew this ought to be his father's kill.

Perhaps he'd just looked at it for too long and his memory had warped, but he was sure that, despite the mummification and slow rot of time, the expression had remained since it last had life behind it. It was a unique kind of fear, the one of impending death, and the expression it left on the face was common to all men. Agbaka was well familiar with it – and not just from time spent gazing at the last independent Ibutho king's head. It was an expression he now read on the boy before him. While he had no intention of killing this little Uzian, Agbaka was in no rush to assure him of that. The boy king trembled in the flickering firelight. Not everyone was so fond of finding themselves in a room full of mummified kings' heads. Especially kings.

But to call this boy a king? He was short and skinny with barely a body hair to speak of. His face was slight and delicate, and his eyes were bright and untarnished by pain. He spoke with a confidence he had no right to, and while he was doing his best to appear assured and stately, he was just a boy whose balls had barely dropped, looking at a man who could crush his neck in one hand. He imagined this child couldn't even lift Idà Owurọ, Agbaka's great sword, let alone cleave a head from its neck. No amount of beauty or charisma could undo the ultimate state of power in this room. Or the world outside it.

'Do you know who that is?' Agbaka asked, pointing at one of the more shrivelled faces.

'No, Emperor Agbaka, I don't,' said the boy, sounding almost apologetic.

'That is King Na'od, the last king of Zufani to defy Obare. This one?'

'No, Emperor. I'm sorry.'

'Don't be sorry, boy. It's my pleasure, no duty, to educate the ignorant on the great history of Obare. This is Mambo Rusvingo of Ijaw. He's over 300 years old. Doesn't look it, does he?' The boy just shook his head. Agbaka moved on. 'This one here is from the Grasslands, back when they had some semblance of civilisation to conquer. He's the last remaining member!' Agbaka always found that funny. 'They used to live in stone towers somewhere east of Zufani. They were… not as easy to defend as they'd hoped. No ocean or valley walls to protect them either.' He chuckled and made sure to look the boy in the eye. And then: 'Do you know which of these is Uzian?' The boy looked shocked by that question; he hurriedly tried to skim over each of the faces, presumably looking for some familial connection.

'No Emperor, I don't.'

'None of them. Not one is from your quiet little nation.' The boy looked almost relieved. 'I quite like this collection, Xola, Boy King. But I've never added to it myself. The greatest of my forefathers added several in their time, my own late father among them.' That expression took hold of the boy's face once more. It was even more severe in one so young. 'You see… I want to do my father proud. You understand that, don't you?'

'I don't know what you're saying, Emperor Agbaka. We are a peaceful people, we pose you no threat.'

That irritated Agbaka. 'You are a stupid boy too far out of your depth. Uzi's very existence is an affront to the rightful balance of power. Your wealth, technology and independence make us look weak and there are cabals of treasonous traitors all over the belt who would have my head for their collection. You embolden them, and no doubt provide sanctuary for their evil schemes. I have no doubt that the very traitors that killed my father and brothers were harboured in your humid little valley.'

'No, no! You're wrong. There are no traitors in—'

'And do you know that?' The boy searched his head, looking for something to sate Agbaka's thirst. Xola's shoulders slumped.

'Please Emperor, my family, my court… we had nothing to do with your father's death. But if anyone in Uzi is found to have been conspiring against the Obare Empire, we will see them appropriately punished.'

'No. That's not good enough.' The little boy's lower lip quivered and his eyes began to water.

'What do you want?'

'I have drawn up a list of demands. Should you fail to meet them, the might of the Obare Empire will crash down the walls of Uzi Valley and the Molili's final passage to the ocean will run red,' he said, enjoying the imagery. 'And boy… I'll leave with my very own trophy to hang in this room. Do you understand?'

He did.

Hall of the fallen kings

The Price Of Peace

The sun was unusually oppressive today. The ripples of the ocean twinkled so brightly that Xola had to squint to make out the path ahead. The air was thick with water that the rains had left overnight and the absence of a typical shoreward breeze left him feeling claustrophobic and sticky. Ordinarily, he loved the delta. The myriad streams that split off from the Molili as it meandered towards the ocean made for a patchwork of possibilities, full of adventure. As a child, he and his friends would come to cool off in one of the pools or conquer an island and claim it as their own for the day. In their imaginary empires, they answered to no one but themselves. Today though, the sense of responsibility was as unbearable as the sun.

Xola and his mother were picking their way across streams and farmland towards the Delta food market. It was a place that evoked less nostalgia for him but still commanded an impressive presence in this otherwise pastoral landscape. The Great-store was the biggest building in Uzi, thick and gnarled Obaseki timber knotted together in intricate interlocking patterns that had then been subsumed by plant life. It was said that each of the foodstuffs of Uzi could be found growing in the foliage; the reality was less romantic than that – rice does not grow on buildings – but it was still an impressive array of flora that spoke to the health of the land. In the months after the rainy season, the Great-store was resplendent with plush new leaves, dripping and juicy, and the country could know the harvest would be good. When the droughts had come some 18 moons past, the colours had faded to a sad, limp brown and spoke to hard days ahead. Today, this microcosm of Uzi's plant life looked thick and thriving, adding to Xola's sense of misery.

The list of demands Agbaka had drawn up was immense and incalculable in cost. He wanted everything. There were the obvious materials: gold, silver, diamonds and other gems, especially uzanite, of which they wanted more than half of the national stores. Then there were things like fabrics and other textiles along with dyes and designs. They wanted building materials – stone and timber – not scarce, admittedly, but not easy to transport to Obare. Then there were the less tangible assets, the truly precious gems of Uzian endeavour: their technologies and insights, hard-won facts about the movement of the stars and the processes of the world. One very keenly stressed stipulation was Uzi's so-called 'fire-sand', the explosive powder they used for their mining operations and fireworks. They also insisted these 'gifts' were accompanied by personnel to educate Obare on their production and uses. And of course, there was food, more than Xola was aware they had. Clearly, they had done their research; the numbers were precise and unforgiving. Xola and his mother had come to their nation's sun-kissed garden to assess just how damaging the losses would be.

The inside of the Great-store was considerably less evocative than its leafy exterior. The impressive carpentry was on better display here, but it was more functional in design. The room was bisected by a long corridor flanked by spacious, two-tiered storage spaces overflowing with sacks of food: grain, rice, maize, beans, lentils, dried fish, cured meat, salt, herbs and spices, each with its own designated space and labelled with the producer's glyph. At the far end was an office of sorts where the store chief and his assistants kept careful records of stocks. Most of the country's produce was distributed throughout Uzi, and this space was for surplus.

'What you are suggesting would be devastating, Your Grace,' said the chief. 'We are in good health now, but the astrologers are certain we are no more than 10 moons from another drought and we've only just recovered from the blight.'

'I'm sorry, Enahoro. I understand and share your reservations, but Obare is in no mood to negotiate,' said Xola's mother. He held her gaze and shook his head.

'I would not be upholding my responsibility if I let this happen. People will die if you do this. Children will be the first to go.'

'People will die if we deny Obare, Chief,' she said.

'This is not my food anyway. It's theirs,' he said, a firm finger extended towards the market outside. 'I serve you, King Xola. You serve them.' His gaze shifted to Xola this time, who'd been doing his best to appear attentive and patient. In reality, his head was away in the Oorun Keep, the faces of Mambo Rusvingo and Yeye kaMpande contorted in eternal anguish, taunting him. He looked up to Chief Enahoro and then to his mother.

'He's right, Xola. They need to hear this from you.' With a look of spiteful acquiescence, Chief Enahoro indicated to the door.

'After you, Your Highness.' Xola's heart sank. He could barely hold a conversation with Khanyishiwa at the moment, let alone convince a crowd of farmers that their lifeline food stores were to be ravaged for the sake of some far-off king's whims. His mother offered an encouraging look, but it did little to settle his nerves.

The heat outside hit him like a charging rhino and his eyes had barely adjusted to the glare of the sun before the sound of the market bell rang out across the square. Business slowed and eyes found their way to the doorframe of the Great-store. Xola's mother stepped back and placed a hand on his shoulder, while Chief Enahoro was near gleeful as he thrust the gathering crowd's attention onto their king. The air found a calm silence, but for the far-off clinking of an Idelta oxen's collar bell as it tended a plough out of view.

'Loyal subjects of Uzi, I am King Xola,' he stammered.

'We know who you are, Xola! Get on with it!' came a heckle from the crowd. Xola winced, closing his eyes and mustering whatever kingly courage he could.

'It is not often I find myself in need of your help. Agbaka the Dauntless, Emperor of the Obare Empire, has made demands of Uzi. If we don't meet them, he will bring war to our country. He is convinced that we harboured the traitors who killed his family and he insists he will raze our nation to the ground if we do not give him what he wants.'

Their silence held this time. He scanned the crowd before him; a mixture of shock and disbelief rippled across their faces. It was only then that he noticed their clothes, ragged and worn, bright colours faded from toil. A little boy's muddy face peered out from behind his mother's legs, not a sandal between them. These were Uzians, but not the same as those who lived further up the valley. Their possessions were few, and each clearly held greater value to them than anything he'd ever owned.

'The vast majority of the wares behind me must go to Obare to sate the Emperor's hunger for revenge. I am asking for your understanding here.'

'And what about the droughts?' came one shout. 'Will you feed us then?' came another.

'You have angered this king and now we will have to pay the price!' Each shout stung.

'I am sorry – we will all be killed if we don't!' 'No one has ever invaded Uzi. It's impossible.' 'Our peace is sacred! It'll never happen!'

'You are lying! You just want more food for your feasts!' The crowd was rumbling now with anger and frustration. Chief Enahoro stood, arms crossed and stiff in his silence. A handful of rotten marula fruit arced its way through the air from the back of the crowd and splattered across Xola's feet; the sweet, rancid smell made him queasy.

'No, please. I have met this man. This is no idle threat!' Xola urged, but it did nothing to soothe the slowly advancing crowd. 'He intends to hang my head–'

'Xola, we should leave now,' muttered his mother in his ear. He didn't need telling twice. As calmly as they could they made their way through the crowd, who jeered and shouted at them as they went. Xola kept his head down. When they were free, he turned to his mother.

'I don't know what to do, mother.' 'Yes you do, Xola.'

'But... people will die. They have nothing down here.'

'The cost of war is too great. It is difficult for us to grasp in Uzi, but... nothing is worth that. These are the responsibilities of a king.'

'My father never had to steal from his own people.'

Her face was tinged with sadness. 'No,' she admitted, 'but his reign was not without suffering. I'm sorry this has fallen to you, Xola, but we cannot make demands of the world. It makes them of us.'

Agbaka seeks counsel from his council

Violence

The crowd erupted as Agbaka entered the seething cauldron that was, at this moment, the capital's immense amphitheatre. He hated it. Of all the supposed privileges of ruling, mindless adulation was one of his least favourite. He did not seek power to be loved; that was not what kings were for.

He was not so foolish as to dismiss the raucous atmosphere as meaningless though. These games were to form the centrepiece of the new high-sun solstice festival: Day of the Dauntless, created – and named – in his honour. Again, it was not an honour he sought, but his advisors had insisted it would be a good way to sustain his nation's new-found morale. 'Well-fed cattle need fewer fences,' as his father liked to say. So, when the crowd began chanting his name, Agbaka raised his hands to the sky and gave them what they wanted: a hero.

The rejuvenated affection was something of an accident, and Xola's fault no less. Obaseki's numbers had been designed to bring Uzi to its knees, reduce the hermit kingdom to a shadow of its gloating self and usher wealth and glory to Obare. But Agbaka had wanted a different outcome. Agbaka had wanted demands that no self-respecting kingdom would capitulate to. Agbaka wanted them to weep at those numbers, and tremble at the new reality they heralded. He had wanted this so much that he intercepted the final list of demands and redrafted them, inflating the numbers even further without any of his council's knowledge. So, when word arrived a few months later of an enormous caravan of Uzian goods a few days out of Obesi, he was astonished. And furious.

His subjects, of course, had a different reaction. Their king had achieved a wondrous and previously unimaginable thing. The days of parsimony and hunger were over for the mountain people. The Lustrous Emperor's 'skilful diplomacy' with the southerners had brought wealth, technology and life-giving sustenance to the precariously positioned people of Obare. Their plateau was fertile but far from prolific, and the immense standing army, stationed in the mountains, was an ever-present drain on resources. This tribute from Uzi, along with the potent technologies that accompanied it, should see them through even the most challenging of seasons. Not since Askia the Great had Obare enjoyed such wealth and prospective stability. Celebrations had erupted in the streets and Agbaka's name could be heard echoing between the Taraba Mountains and beyond. His political advisors suggested he hold a holiday for his people, an official, empire-wide jubilation to mark the upcoming high-sun solstice. It could recur on an annual basis, a true legacy.

So he did. But it was not the legacy that he wanted. None of the gifts in the Uzian wagons could be hung in the Hall of Fallen Kings. His council were satisfied that their terms had been met and war had been averted, but Agbaka still found himself struggling to sleep through the night, his mind racing to devise innovative ways for an army to pour down valley walls. No parades or pageantry could sate this hunger.

The games did have the potential to provide some temporary relief at least. The main event, the one he insisted he'd take part in, was a tournament of ọpá ija, a martial combat sport in which competitors wield long, supple sticks. Its origins lay a good distance from the Obare Plateau, in some wide jungle valley south of the Zufani Kingdom. But, in the generations since its originating tribe's subsumption into the greater Obare Empire, it had become his people's favourite sport, a blood-thirsty reality Agbaka was happy to sponsor.

The game had not always been something he'd enjoyed. It was first introduced to him by his brothers, Idemudia and Itua, some seven and nine years his senior. They took great pleasure in practising their new moves on their small and insignificant little brother. He looked back now and knew he owed them a debt of gratitude. It hardened his body and soul and gave him plenty of motivation to practise himself. By the time he became a man, Agbaka was more than capable of cracking their skulls; unfortunately, they knew better than to brandish their ada around him by then. He made a silent toast to their memory and drank the half-gourd of cow's blood, handing it back empty to the medicine man at his side. He hoped they were looking up to him today. He hoped they knew what he had become, the man they had helped make.

He felt the last drops of the warm sweet liquid fall from the corners of his mouth as he bared his teeth and marched towards the centre of the ring. At his own request, he'd been paired with one of the higher-ranking champions, a man by the name of Takala Zagwe – notable enough to impress the crowd but not enough to confuse their allegiance; while he was more than comfortable being disliked, it was not something he felt the need to court. This elephant of a man before him was no doubt powerful, but Agbaka was quick – and clever too. Takala hunched over, pounded the ground before him and glared at Agbaka. He was under strict instructions not to hold back. The game was simple: he who submits loses.

There was a moment of stillness as the crowd held their breath. Agbaka held his combatant's gaze. A horn rang out across the arena and Agbaka moved first. He lurched forward at pace, watching carefully for Takala's response. The enormous man's tree-stump feet shuffled right, so Agbaka dropped his shoulder as if to move that way. Takala took the bait and swung down sharply. Agbaka launched himself off his right foot into the air just in time. A puff of pink sand erupted from the ground as the ija fell past his right shoulder and into the dirt. Without hesitation, Agbaka struck back: an almighty backhand straight to the man's temple. The crowd cheered as Agbaka spun on his toes and found himself standing at Talaka's flank as he dizzily regained his balance. The crowd's champion did not hesitate and launched a brutal two-handed swing across Takala's upper back. The connection was good, and blood wept from the wound, but Takala found his footing quickly and returned with a rapid outstretched right arm that hit Agbaka's thigh. Agbaka pulled back and found his footing once more, awaiting Takala's response.

Internally, Agbaka marvelled at the ease with which his body navigated this game, representative of his affinity for combat in general. His brothers played their role in driving him to develop these skills, and much of that ability was hard-won. But there was something more ineffable at work too. He felt this was what he had been built for. It was more than strength and speed; his capacity for pain and eye for weakness built on these skills, and the hunger within him was an endless source of ruthless vigour. They must be traits inherited from his mother. Although he never knew her – and the stories spoke of someone gentle and gracious – they could not have come from his father. His father was a great man and a kind-hearted ruler, with barely a hint of severity or violence in his being. Lacking these traits was what ultimately led to his death. The strong will always rise to the top and the weak will serve or die, Agbaka concluded. It was the natural way of things. His own ascension spoke to that.

Even as these thoughts cluttered his mind, his body seemed to move without prompting. Ducking and diving, slugging and swiping – Agbaka could almost sit back and watch it happen. He was meant for this and thrived here. The rest of the exchange passed in a blur of ferocity and grace. Takala got one or two half-decent body hits, but Agbaka bested him at almost every turn. He focused on the head and ankles to hurt his opponent's balance, and Takala fell on several occasions. But, credit to the man, he found his feet after each. Battered and bloodied, his combatant slowed, and Agbaka could hit with greater precision. He finally thumped Takala's left eye, the giant stumbled back, yelling in pain. He surrendered; he didn't want to lose them both.

The crowd took a moment to find their voice, the brutality of their King and Emperor's victory surprising even them. But eventually, they cheered louder than they had all day. Even Agbaka relished it. It meant they understood. His strength and power mirrored that of the empire he presided over – and elevated it to new heights. He was their rightful ruler and he'd lead them to their rightful future. They loved it.

As he left the arena, Agbaka's mind turned to that weak and fearful kingdom of Uzi, yet to bow the knee. It was an affront to all that was right, and he could stand it no longer. By the time he'd arrived back to the Oorun Keep, his eyes settled on the south-western horizon once more, his mind was made up: *Uzi must fall.*

Romance

Xola couldn't sleep. He rolled over in his bed for what felt like the hundredth time. He knew it was not his position in bed that disturbed him, though. His eyes fell to the window, the full moon's light streaming through the window and the noise of crickets crooning with extraordinary verve flooded through. But that wasn't the problem either.

He hadn't slept well since he'd left for Obare, all those moons ago. The mummified face of Yeye kaMpande still haunted him and the knot of anxiety that Agbaka had crammed into his chest had only gotten worse as time passed. Xola had hoped that, by the time the tribute had arrived in Obare, he'd feel soothed. But it wasn't to be. He couldn't help but worry that they'd forgotten something or missed some specific stipulation – the slightest oversight could be used as cause to invade. He ran the checks through his head over and over but always failed to convince himself.

The stress of preparing the caravan of goods had left its mark on his turbulent inner life too. His experience at the Great Store had prepared him for a struggle, but the reality had been much worse, even outside of the delta. The engineers and innovators in charge of Uzi's famed firesand were incredibly protective of their creation. They insisted that, in the wrong hands, this innovation had the potential to cause profound suffering and looked for ways to diminish its power or send some false alternative, but Xola couldn't allow it. It had made for a bruising exchange. The fight over the food was worse though and ended with the Ibhotwe Guard being sent in to forcibly extract the stock from Enahoro. It was a miracle that no one got hurt. Uzi's farmers and artisans responded to the upheaval in whatever ways they could. They began insisting on their right to hoard whatever they produced, their usual distributive ethos disintegrating into self-preservation and spite. The farmers were especially vehement in their refusal to allow what remained of their goods to leave their community. Luxuries like meat were among the first to be kept for the delta alone. Xola hadn't eaten meat for a month.

And while all of that conspired to hinder his rest, it was not what kept him awake this night. No, tonight it was the thought of Khanyishiwa. It was not as though his other troubles were not plaguing him; instead, they had found a perfect focal point in his flickering romantic flame. She was from the delta and her family were rice farmers. He worried that she harboured their malcontent; that she, like all the rest, held him responsible for the chaos and pain. Things hadn't been going well before that either. All the anxiety of the political intrigue he found himself at the centre of had reduced him to a shell of his once charismatic self. He could barely muster the charm to thank his cooks at breakfast, let alone engage in courtship. So, when he passed her on his way to the council halls earlier today, he panicked, averted his gaze and ran away like some terrified meerkat. The embarrassment of that moment had curdled within him and churned through his mind making sleep a practical impossibility.

Xola leapt out of bed. There was no point in sitting here feeling sorry for himself. He had to undo it and undo it now.

Khanyishiwa had probably left their 'encounter' this afternoon with the conclusion that he was no longer interested in her or didn't like her or something equally untrue. He couldn't just keep turning in his bed waiting for her to forget him. He had to do something. He threw on some clothes, combed his hair and prayed for his heart to slow. Before he knew it, he was already tip-toeing out of the palace, past the sleeping Ibhotwe Guard and down the central thoroughfare of Uzi City. By the time he arrived at the food shop she worked and lived in, the excitement had overrun the fear; he felt almost confident.

The window was just about low enough for him to pull himself up to and peer in. Sure enough, there she was, sound asleep. The shaft of moonlight that poured in over his head framed her face perfectly. In shadow, Auntie Nongqawuse, the ill-tempered proprietor of this fine establishment, snored just off to her left. He thought for a moment before returning to the ground, then gathered a handful of pebbles and hoisted himself back up. His aim was less than perfect but true enough to avoid the gargling crone in the corner. Eventually, he made good contact and

Khanyishiwa woke up.

Blearily, she blinked up at him, squinting as her eyes adjusted and worked hard to discern features within his silhouette. He waved as recognition flickered across her face. She mouthed his name with a quizzical expression. He nodded vigorously and beckoned her over. She scowled before checking her patron was still sleeping. With a dancer's delicacy, she picked her way across the floor to meet him at the window. 'What are you doing here?!' There was more than a hint of irritation to her whispered hisses. It twinged within him, but he was in too deep now.

'I... err... thought you might want to take a walk?!' he said with a grin.

'You thought I might want to take a walk?' 'Yes! Exactly!'

'It's the middle of the night!'

'It's a full moon! It hardly counts.' She raised an eyebrow. 'Come on. King's orders!' he added, cheekily.

Her mouth twitched open in search of a riposte, but her face softened before she found anything. The knot in his chest loosened, and Khanyishiwa's eyes twinkled. She let out a silent sigh of acquiescence and hoisted herself up through the window. Xola stepped back and offered a hand for her to climb down. She made a point of not taking it.

'A matter of state, is it?' she said, in a toying manner.

'Oh, yes. Utmost importance.' They made their way up the valley towards the waterfall.

'And how can I serve my country this night?' The soft rumble of the waterfall's tumbling water, carried on the wind, wafted towards them, drawing their gaze up. The thin mist of spray formed a halo above the cliff top, shimmering in the moonlight. Xola was quietly smug – it was as though he'd planned it.

'It's the stars, you see. We just need to make sure they're all there.'

'Oh really? You're worried someone stole them and carted them off to Obare?' she said with a chuckle. Xola winced and stopped in his tracks. That didn't take long.

'… I… I'm sorr–'

'Xola – I'm teasing you! You're too easy. Consider it payback for waking me up.' He let go a laugh, somewhat stifled by the genuine relief.

'I don't blame you.'

'Really?'

'No. Some do. But not me. At least, not for that.' 'For what then?'

'For ignoring me this afternoon! In fact, for ignoring me since you got back from Obare!' He felt a wave of nauseating shame wash over him.

'I'm sorry. It's all just been… It's been horrible, Khanyishiwa.' She took him by the hand. 'I'm sorry I've been avoiding you, I've just not known what to do with myself. I… I think, I don't know how to be the king and Xola at the same time. Do you understand what I mean?'

She chuckled. 'No, not at all! But it's okay.' She smiled at him. He smiled back. 'I'm just glad it's not something I did! I was worried you were too busy being a king to be interested in someone like me.'

'No! No! Not at all! Khanyishiwa – you are all I am interested in. All I have ever been interested in. But this stuff with Emperor Agbaka… it doesn't matter whether I'm interested or not. People will die if–'

She cut him off. 'Stop. Don't finish that sentence. Go back to the bit where I'm all that you are interested in. I'm much more interested in *that.*'

Xola felt very bashful all of a sudden. It was definitely better than 'anxious' but stifled him just the same. A strange, pretty silence hung between them. Xola rubbed the back of his neck. Khanyishiwa ducked her gaze.

'So… about these stars,' he said. 'Yes?'

'Well, there's a lot of them, you see. We need to start counting if you're going to be back before the Nongqawuse wakes up!'

Khanyishiwa laughed properly this time. 'I think she's probably as bad as that Emperor Agbaka!'

'No. She's worse.' Xola laughed too.

There was a moment when his mind drifted back to Obare and the Hall of Fallen Kings. The thought threatened to linger. But then he looked around at Khanyishiwa again and remembered everything was actually okay. Nongqawuse really was the worst of their worries at that moment. And then, for the first time in a long time, Xola really didn't mind being awake.

Bloodshed And Burning

The final shafts of sunlight faded into shadow as Agbaka wound his way down the long staircase. The guards scrambled to attention as he passed, startled by their emperor's unannounced presence. He marched past prisoners of all shapes and sizes. Some were familiar. Others were clearly not important enough to have left a mark on his memory. Eventually, he came to the end of the corridor, down one more flight of stairs and arrived at a hall of empty cells.

Empty bar one.

It had taken no more than a week since the Day of the Dauntless for the wave of conviction to finally break. He sought no further counsel. He called a meeting of his War Cabinet purely to instruct his First Blade, First Spear and First Shield to muster their forces at the northern passage of the Obare Plateau; Imaghodo was to send word to Zufani. At the first light of the twenty-first day from high-sun, they would depart for Uzi.

While he neither sought nor needed approval from his military leaders, it was customary (and advisable) to hear from the seers before embarking on a military campaign. Agbaka knew he would not be dissuaded from his course, but an appreciation of the omens could only help guide his strategy and refine his timeline. First was Imaghodo, who was his usual combination of deferential, pathetic and placatory. Agbaka watched as the man sweated his way through an awkward and shameless approval of his plans. Imaghodo was the closest his palace had to a pacifist, but his preference for confrontation avoidance took precedence. 'The Obare Empire is the mightiest it has ever been, and the great bounty and the military innovations it has led to can only aid an uncomplicated and complete victory,' and so on. It was nothing more or less than he expected from this worm of a man. It was a formality really, a ritual.

There was a second seer though, one Agbaka had not seen or spoken to since long before his father died. Even then, it was at the late Emperor's side. Ojebun had never liked Agbaka and had made no effort into hiding that fact. His father placed great faith in the seer's advice though, which was the only thing that had saved him from execution. His father was a much better reader of people than he was, so Agbaka did not take his commendation lightly. Instead of the chop, Ojebun had spent Agbaka's emperorship deep in the dungeons of the keep. Agbaka had made sure to keep him well fed and well looked after but had denied him access to anyone with influence. Today was different.

In the caverns of the Oorun Keep, Agbaka approached this lonely cell. The soft rumble of the Molili passing deep beneath their feet was the only thing holding back a dead silence.

'Good morning, Ojebun.' The wrinkled old man sat on the flat stone that doubled as his bed. His eyes were closed, his hair massed in white dreadlocks. His beard was neatly pleated with beads weighing it down, and he looked skinnier than Agbaka remembered. But no less sure of himself. He opened his eyes slowly and turned to meet Agbaka's gaze. He was completely unsurprised. Agbaka felt a wave of unease.

'Is it morning? Already?' Agbaka didn't answer. 'You have come about Uzi.'

'We depart at dawn, five days from now.'

'Ah. That came around quickly.' Agbaka didn't know what that meant.

'Tell me what you see, old man.' Ojebun's stare did not break.

'You must not do this, Agbaka. Nothing but bloodshed and burning awaits you in Uzi. I see a darkness covering the land and your army shattered. Those that survive will retreat to the wilderness, only to be eaten by animals. I see the great Dauntless Emperor's head on a spike.' Agbaka's heart quickened. He forced a chuckle.

'And who will do this, Ojebun? What army?'

'Don't you see, Emperor? *The Uzians*. Men. Women.

Children. *All of them.*'

Agbaka laughed truly this time. 'You've gone mad, old man. The years of incarceration have not been kind to your mind.'

'The rainmaker who doesn't know what he's doing will be found out by the lack of clouds. Your father failed to listen to me only once and it cost him his life. Do not make the same mistake.'

Agbaka's eyes narrowed. He'd had enough of this nonsense riddle-making. He turned on his heels and headed back towards the steps.

'Stupid old fool,' he muttered as he wound his way back towards the sun.

The Third Son

Asaba was flooded by emotions so profound he could hardly keep his knees from buckling. His heart was being wenched in two directions, and he seemed to feel both at their fullest. The gift was truly a blessing from the ancestors, but the price was almost unfathomable.

He had wanted a girl, but the boy in his arms was beautiful beyond compare. The first two looked much more like him, and they had cried all through their first days. This little one had barely mustered up a whimper. And he looked just like his mother – her final gift, he thought, a living reminder of her beauty and grace.

Imaghodo had been of great comfort in grief. He was a great friend, whose benignity radiated, warming all around him. His reading of the omens and expectations for the boy's future on the other hand had been his usual mix of gentleness and pointlessness. Something about 'great success with the softer sex' and 'a taste for fine foods'.

He expected his meeting with Ojebun to be quite different though. If two wise men always agree, then there is no need for one of them, he thought. The sage had never had much capacity for clemency or tenderness, but his insight and guidance were of the highest order. He was a man you sought out at your peril but avoided at your ruin. Asaba looked into his third son's eyes as they flickered open from soft slumber, and his knees quivered once more. Ojebun would surely see the boy for the blessing he clearly was.

Ojebun liked to meet outside. He said the winds only spoke truth. He had chosen his station well; Obare was not known for its clement weather. The roof of the Oorun Keep was kept unadorned, save for a few statues. Better it was, Asaba felt, for witnessing the immense view of the plateau behind and the Laruba Expanse ahead. It was most certainly windy.

'Ojebun. How goes it?'

'My deepest condolences, Kind Emperor. Adebisi was a blessing from the ancestors. It can only have been at their behest that she was called to join them.' Perhaps he'd been unkind in his expectations. There was some comfort in those words.

'Thank you, Ojebun. I will never recover from her loss. I only thank the ancestors that they saw fit to leave me with a reminder of her beauty. I'd... like you to meet Agbaka.' Asaba stepped forward and held out his third son for Ojebun to see. The seer caught Asaba's eye and held it sternly. He did not look at the child. 'Tell me. What do the winds say to you?'

There was no hesitation. The seer's face darkened.

'You must know what they say of a child that brought death to its mother, Asaba.' Asaba's heart quickened.

'No... I don't. And I don't much care about what they say.' Ojebun maintained his unforgiving expression.

'Yes, superstitions, for the most part. But I do not deal in superstitions. I deal in truth. And I tell you this, Kind Emperor: this boy must not live beyond his first year.'

'What? He is sickly?'

'No, Emperor. He is in full health and will remain so, unless by actions of your own. They are actions I must advise you to take.'

'I don't understand, Ojebun.'

'Asaba. This child will bring death and destruction to countless people. He will be responsible for an era of suffering this world will not soon forget. I am sorry to tell you this, my friend.'

'You're wrong. You must be wrong. He is only the third son, third in line. How can he...?'

'Heed my warning, Good Emperor. Your life and empire depend on it.'

★★★

With each swing, Idà Owurọ became more and more difficult to heave into the air. It had been his sword since he'd learned to fight, but those lessons had been intentionally brief. This war, on the other hand, had drawn out long beyond what was anticipated, and this battle had seen two dawns. Asaba's body was not intended for this. He was a skilled statesman and intelligent manager of people and resources, but a sword swung heavily in his hands.

But they just kept coming. Individually, they were far from skilled warriors. Peasants, most probably. A combination of farmers and fishermen, carpenters and trackers. Each with a life, a mother, a father. Perhaps, even children. Some of them basically were children. Their strength was in numbers, so Ibutho training focused on movement, formations and collective intimidation rather than actual combat. The main military strategy seemed to lie in wearing their opposition's appetite for killing. Asaba hadn't much of a taste for it to begin with.

He didn't ask for this campaign. He had great respect – affection even – for the Ibutho tribes. They were a fiercely free and proud people, as unbounded as the vast plains and rolling hills of their region, and almost as untameable. Asaba was old enough to remember a time before their confederation when they were too busy killing each other in territorial disputes to cause much trouble for any other people of the world. But Yeye kaMpande was an organiser like no other. He had a vision of a united Ibutho people, self-governing but by no one in particular. It was a vision of a society that even he, Asaba, the sole ruler of the largest empire in Ultro history, found rather beautiful. But his council saw a threat. The well-organised Ibutho people could hold their own even against the combined forces of Obare. Better to strike fast before a coherent military doctrine could take hold. It was a plan championed most vocally by his youngest son. In fact, when his council came to a decision on the campaign, Agbaka was intimidating in his capacity for military planning. He'd barely left Asaba's side since, excitedly sharing his latest strategic innovations.

His affinity for war did not stop there. Nor did his proximity to his father. The follow-through of yet another swing through another son of Ibutho, saw Asaba's sword crash into the earth. He took a moment to catch his breath and clear the sweat from his brow. Even with his head bowed and eyes to the ground, he could hear the clatter of Agbaka's sword as it extinguished another life. His son was grunting gleefully as it did so. It would have been more unpleasant if his efficiency was not hastening the end of this interminable skirmish.

'Father! I think this one's for you.' Asaba did not want to look up. He didn't want to see the thrill on his son's face or whatever 'prize' he'd acquired for him. But he was as afraid of getting on the wrong side of Agbaka as the rest of his court. So, he looked up. The boy peered out at his father, grinning from behind a wet, red mask. Asaba assumed none of the blood was his own. At his feet was the great and mighty Yeye kaMpande, reduced to human rubble. He sagged and swayed under Agbaka, who held him by the thick fur and beaded leather straps that hung from his shoulders. He was barely conscious. One more swing, Asaba thought.

***

He woke with a start. The sound of shouts and clashing swords echoed down the corridor. He sat up and, as if by instinct, turned to wake his wife. He was met, as he was every waking moment, by the reality of her loss. At least now, whatever was happening outside their bed-chamber posed no threat to her. Footsteps announced the arrival of someone at his door. It swung open at the hand of Kaina Kimba, Asaba's First Shield. He was panicked and panting. Asaba didn't need any further cue. He rose from the bed and threw on a robe.

'Chief?' Asaba asked as his head of security caught his breath.

'Your sons, Emperor…' 'What? My sons what?'

'Akoi and Askia… they've been murdered. We need to leave now.' The blood drained from Asaba's face.

'And Agbaka?!'

'We can't find him.' 'Find him. Quickly!'

'I have men searching. I cannot leave your side.'

Asaba dashed to the wall to retrieve his great sword from its fixture. He turned, Idà Owurọ in hand, just in time to see Kania Kimba's throat slit. Blood wept from his neck as he fell limply to the floor. Asaba's eyes were too busy bearing witness to his friend's final breath to register the man wielding the knife. At least, initially. He brought a second hand to his sword's hilt and raised his gaze.

'Agbaka...' His third and only living son adjusted his grip on the knife and advanced. Asaba raised his sword and found his stance, holding his ground as best as he could. Agbaka watched his father's footing carefully and lowered his body. There was a moment of stillness. Their eyes met and Asaba searched for the little boy he'd held in his arms all those years ago, or for any last glimpse of his late wife behind them. But there was nothing. Only focus.

All the strength fell from Asaba's body and Idà Owurọ clattered to the floor. He fell to his knees and sobbed.

'My boy. My sweet boy.'

Agbaka killing the guard on the way to kill his Father

Enogie, High Priestess Of The Moon

Uzi was in turmoil. The dust kicked up after the great tribute had just about settled when news of Obare's mobilisation reached the valley. It was barely a month later when their arrival was announced with a terrifying bang. Scouts and engineers were quick to confirm suspicions: Agbaka had taken Uzian fire-sand and found a way to launch rocks from bronze tubes with its explosive force. Fortunately, their projectiles had met only rock so far, but their aim was improving. Xola wasn't sure Agbaka was even trying to hit, so much as to intimidate the people of the valley below. If so, he was succeeding.

News of Obare's mighty army amassed on the walls of Uzi Valley spread like wildfire in high-sun among Xola's people. To the northwest, some ten thousand foot soldiers, the feared Obare Lancers and an array of auxiliary units were camped and awaited orders. A week or so later, their allies from Zufani, replete with the greatest archers in the known world and siege weapons to boot, lined up along the valley's south-eastern wall. Combined, it was a force capable of razing Uzi several times over, and his people knew it.

Already, responsibility for this catastrophe had been laid at Xola's feet. He had angered the Dauntless Emperor. He created more problems in negotiation. And it was he who then failed to give Agbaka what he wanted. All that pain and suffering he'd rendered among his people, only to have war arrive anyway. He knew that wasn't how it was, but, in his darker moments, he couldn't help but share his people's disdain.

The council was no better composed than his subjects. Their crisis meetings had been a mess of accusations, panic and disagreement. Should they surrender? Should they seek military aid from Obare's oppressed? Ibutho was only a few weeks' ride away, and Ijaw not much further. Or they could evacuate and flee, seek refuge in the Abe-okuta or Southern Plains. The prevailing opinion among the elders, however, was that they should simply accept their fate and surrender.

Xola was paralysed. All he could think about was his mother and Khanyishiwa – seemingly the only two people in Uzi with any capacity for calm. Khanyishiwa was a blessing. She was as terrified as everyone else, but somehow she managed to talk him down from his misanthropic outbursts and pessimistic acquiescence. Even if she could not dissuade him from his feelings of guilt and fear, she helped him feel like there was something worth soldiering on for.

His mother had taken a different approach. She'd left Xola's side and buried herself in Uzi's archive vaults looking for answers from the nation's past, convinced that explanations of Uzi's 'sacred peace' had been hidden away but not forgotten. A half-moon since the first warning shot from the valley walls, she emerged with a cloak and a plan.

The cloak belonged to Xola's great-great-great-grandfather, Urughu. He was not a figure Xola knew much about, but the Uzi of today, Uzi of the New Moon, was said to be his legacy. The cloak was midnight blue with a silver thread trim, a thin crescent moon embroidered onto its back. It was heavy and musty, but it fit Xola perfectly. He felt safer in its embrace. It was his mother's directive that made him nervous. Her tone was unwavering.

'You must seek counsel from Enogie, the High Priestess of the Moon.' He hadn't heard that title since he was a child. Enogie was the oldest of a dying order that dated back to a past age. 'The temple caves up on the ledges by Inyanga Waterfall. You'll find her there. Go. Hurry!'

She could have said anything at that moment and he'd have done it, but something about the way his mother spoke, or perhaps, the mention of Enogie, prompted a pang of hope. He ran.

There was a narrow staircase carved into the rock face that zigzagged up towards the ruins of the Inyanga Temple, the final preserve of Uzi's mystic order. Xola dashed his way towards the overgrown ledges, kept damp by spray from the waterfall. Following the remains of a slippery and moss-covered path, he passed statues of proud soldiers and statesmen in various degrees of dismemberment. The rock face was broken up by high-arched caves echoing with the squeaks of water swallows. Two shot past, aiming for a fish that had failed to avoid the fall. Some of the caves had pillars cut into their walls, and Uzian brickwork partitioned spaces inside. These were the temples of an ancient age steeped in darkness, and not somewhere any of those on the valley floor stepped lightly. Xola looked back at the blood-red sky over Uzi as the sun dipped towards the horizon.

He made his way into one of the bigger caves, which opened to a subterranean complex of corridors and cavernous halls. It was drier and less noisy than the ledge but still somehow overgrown with rare plants that thrived in the darkness. His path was lit by a green glow that emanated from mosses and lichens found nowhere but on these walls.

'Hello?' Xola called as the labyrinth began to look unforgiving.

'This way, King Xola,' came the response, echoing down one of the corridors in front of him. He followed the voice to a further inner chamber, where he was confronted with the sight of a hunched figure, draped in the same luminescent greenery as the walls, her furrowed face up-lit by its glow. Her footsteps were followed by the clack of wood on stone as she sought to stabilise herself with a staff, her bony fingers gripping its gnarled, bulbous head.

'Enogie?'

'Yes, King Xola. Although, I might have mistaken you for ancestor Urughu in that cloak.'

'You knew him?' She just smiled. 'The armies of Obare are amassed on the walls of the valley. They will attack–'

'At dawn,' she said. 'You must move quickly!' 'But move where? What can I do?'

'Tell your mother and the elders to evacuate the young children. They will be safe in these caves. Everyone else must find tools for killing – anything that might work as a weapon.'

He shivered at the thought. 'And me?'

'You must seek the Black Equinox. You will need the heart of a two-headed goat, the head of an owl and the eyes of an orphaned eagle. I have the latter here. The rest, you will find on your way.'

'What is the Black Equinox? And how will I find it?'

'That's what the cloak is for. Make for the Abe-okuta. Asi will know which path to take. She will find you.' She handed him a small vial of preserved eagle eyes, blessed him to ward off the evil spirits that lurked in the forest, and sent him on his way.

Xola's head was swimming. The Black Equinox? He dashed down the steps from the caves and leapt on Asi, waiting at the cliff's foot. His mother was quick to help source the remaining offerings, and before long, he was following a gully from the far north-western edge of the Uzi Delta. Silently, Asi slinked around the furthest reaches of the Obare encampment towards the forbidding treeline ahead.

Black ebony, sapele and iroko trees stooped and swayed in the shoreward breeze, forced up at pace from the delta below. Asi sniffed her way around the path that led into the interior but chose not to take it. Further down, a white, star-drop orchid hung from the bough of a limba tree. That was enough for her. She ducked her head and proceeded through the thick green undergrowth and into the forest.

She was careful and slow as she picked her way through the shrubs and scrub; Xola ducked occasionally to avoid a hanging vine or low branch. Eventually, Asi found her way into a small clearing dappled in the half-moon light. The carcass of a mighty afrormosia tree lay across its centre, surrounded by saplings vying for a slice of the sky above. Asi stopped and sat; Xola took the cue and dismounted. He approached the fallen giant which had begun its journey back to the forest's soil, the scent of its slow decay hung in the air.

A twig snapped somewhere in the distance. Xola swung around suddenly aware of just how alone he was. He wasn't sure he'd ever been more alone.

Until he wasn't. The wing beats were audible first, and before long, the air they stirred up could be felt floating over his skin. He watched as a great black bird, a kind he'd never seen before, landed on the fallen trunk before him. It had the look of an eagle but with a shining white spot between its eyes. The bird flung open its wings to reveal a canopy of star-like twinkling underneath, more silver white spots that glowed with otherworldly grace.

Xola knew it immediately: this was the Black Equinox.

Xola's girlfriend, sad as he's leaving to seek the Black Equinox

Amira

Uzi was in turmoil. Queen Nomski's decree had sent shivers of terror to the very heart of valley society. The arrival of her enforcers in the streets had only stoked the flames further. Azen and Oso alike were scared for their lives. The Queen's father had died mysteriously half a moon previously, having received threats from a witch doctor from whom he'd seized land in the delta. She had come to power full of anger, hatred and paranoia. She would not rest until every sorcerer in the land was dead.

Urughu ran up the valley and past a hanging corpse: the royal court's healer, he concluded, based on the rich, distinctive silks her body was draped in and the Uzanite gem that hung between her eyes. Even that kind of magic was something to be feared, apparently. He'd managed to avoid the Ibhotwe Guard so far, but this high up the valley, they were sure to be nearby. He ducked round the side of a house and worked his way through shadows before braving the open one last time to arrive at Amira's home.

'Amira,' he called out, in as hushed a tone as he could. 'We need to get out of here.' He peeled back the reed curtain and ducked inside. The room was dark, but the faint shimmer of silver light gave her away: hiding under a draped table. He lifted the cloth; the young girl cowered in the corner. 'Don't worry, I'm here. You're safe for now, but we need to go. Now.' He grabbed her by the hand and moved out into the night.

The river would be safest, he felt, and quietest, so they headed straight for the banks of the Mollili. A small canoe sat waiting and he ushered Amira in. Urughu kicked off from the side and buried his companion in his cloak, making sure to keep any of her glow from seeping out, which he knew would give them away in an instant. The movement of the water was enough to keep them going; strokes of the oar would not be worth the noise they made. Head held low, Urughu kept his eyes on the banks as they slid past. Anyone who did notice them was too busy fleeing a burning building or hiding themselves to care about Urughu and his quiet cargo.

They drifted silently towards the delta.

★★★

Urughu followed the trail of star-drop orchids through the thick foliage of the Abe-okuta, making sure to keep low and quiet, wary of being followed. He ducked under branches and leapt over the half-eaten carcass of a forest giraffe before the thin vein of path he was following was interrupted by a bark-covered barricade. This familiar wall of wood was in fact a buttress root from the tall afrormosia tree it connected to. He rapped his knuckles on the section in front of him and waited. After a moment, a knock came back from the other side. He headed for the trunk and pulled back the leaves of a shrub at the base of the tree to reveal a small opening, which he slid through.

He dropped down into the space on the other side of the root, carved into the earth and covered with a truss draped in vegetation to hide the hole beneath. The space opened out into a room, half underground and as big as a small house in the valley. It wasn't much, but space enough for Amira. And it was safe.

'I brought some more knives. I know the ones you were using were getting blunt.'

'Thank you, Urughu,' Amira said.

'And I know you don't get these out here,' he said with a smile. Amira squealed at the sight of fish, 'Caught off the delta earlier today.' She gave him a kiss on the cheek as thanks.

'Don't they wonder where you keep disappearing to?' 'Yes, they do. But no one knows.'

'I'm not worried about me.'

'Don't worry at all. I don't spend time with anyone that would harm either of us if they did know you were here. In fact, they'd be overjoyed to know that there is still at least one of the Azen still alive.' Amira's face fell at the thought.

'Things can't stay like this forever, Urughu. One day, someone will find out and they'll torture you for harbouring me.'

'Not if we succeed. The resistance is growing. Nomski can only hold us off for so long.' Amira's glow flickered with uncertainty.

'I worry about you, that's all. She'll crack down. She'll come for their leader first.'

'We're stronger than you know, Amira. And we're nearly ready to make our move.'

Her face was full of fear and trepidation. She swallowed before looking her protector in the eye. 'When the time comes, you will call for me, won't you? I can help you.'

'Amira, you are our strategy.'

***

Urughu liked the cloak. The silver ring that sat on his head was a little less flattering, but sadly cloaks didn't make a king. The 'Age of the New Moon' they called it. He felt the mystic order might be getting ahead of themselves by calling it an 'age'. It had only just started and it may only last a few moons! Whatever the case, Urughu had a job to do in healing his nation. Never in all their history had so much Uzian blood been spilt. Whatever the Age of the New Moon amounted to, peace would be its guiding principle.

'I don't think this is the way to achieve that,' said Enogie. 'This started when Nomski banished the Azen. Do not let that be how it ends.'

'I am not banishing anyone, High Priestess,' Urughu replied. 'It is what our people want. They have already seen enough bloodshed. Amira understands.' Amira sat quietly. It was not her way to assert herself.

'It's not just the Black Equinox you'll need to force from this valley, Urughu, but the memory of her and what she made possible here.'

'Then so be it. Uzi is a place of peace.' He turned to speak to Amira directly this time. 'I do not want my people to wield your power ever again.' Enogie just shook her head.

'You are short-sighted, Urughu. Such power does offer the temptation of violence, but it does not guarantee it. And what if violence comes from outside of Uzi? Without Amira's power, this valley is defenceless.'

He knew that much. 'Violence begets violence, Enogie. You may call it short-sighted, but I call it drawing a line in the sand, bringing an end to the cycle. We will show this world what peace begets.'

'You are a great and noble leader, King Urughu. But violence is a part of nature. It will return to Uzi one day.' She was right and he knew it.

'But it will not be because of me or the Black Equinox.'

'And what says she?' The eyes of the council all turned to Amira. She had been following the conversation closely.

She thought for a moment.

'I will leave. I do not want to be the cause of any more violence.' Murmurs of approval rippled across the room. The priestesses remained silent. Amira stood up and headed for the door.

'Then it is decided,' said Enogie.

After the applause and adulation, Urughu made a swift exit and caught up with Amira a little way down the valley.

'I'm sorry, Amira. The old ways of Uzi are gone.' She offered a comforting look.

'I'll not go far, My King. Should Uzi need me again, you know where to find me.'

Xola meets the Black Equinox

Fury

The night had been long and quiet. Agbaka hadn't slept. He never slept on nights like this.

The stillness of the air and the camp's quiet calm gave him space to find focus. All the decisions had been made; the army had their orders. There was no more work to be done. His responsibility at this moment extended no further than the inside of his mind. At dawn, the future of Obare and the entire Laruba Expanse would be written, and he was the author. He thought of his father; his death would not be in vain.

Agbaka stood alone at the valley's edge, his toes gripping its jagged ledge. The sheer drop invigorated him. It was a feeling of neither fear nor comfort, a delicate balance between life and death, an inner edge he craved more than anything in the world. He peered down at the flickering lights of the city below, soon to be extinguished. They were matched by the twinkling of the heavens above, equally doomed by the impending dawn. He stood, stilly, watching the stars begin to fade as the pink shift of the new day crept westwards and snuffed out each of them, one by one. By the time the first rays of sunlight sliced their way through the horizon, he had been joined by the vanguard he was to lead. None stood as near the edge as he. Finally, the sun broke free of the horizon and all eyes turned to Agbaka for his mark.

He took one more breath and dropped.

He turned mid-air and grasped behind him; his fingers met with thick, coarse rope netting. He climbed downwards, fast. Looking up, the cliff edge was cluttered with the first wave of soldiers as they reached their feet down to find the net. Like a plague of mountain lizards, they scurried down the walls of Uzi valley, the great rock nets funnelling down to seven points down its north-western wall. Agbaka was leading the descent on point number four and was the first of all seven to reach the bottom. One-handed, he pulled the coiled rope ladder from his belt and attached its top to the fastening point at the net's downward-pointing apex. He kicked the coil out and it tumbled before slapping its final rungs against the buttressing rocks near the valley floor. Already, the rest of his unit had begun to gather above him, so he wasted no time and continued his descent.

As he neared the end of the ladder, Agbaka turned to take note of what awaited him: an old man with a pitchfork. He hastened his arrival with a leap. The old man did his best to look intimidating, waving the rusty implement around in front of him. Agbaka was in no mood for games. He ducked and turned on his toes before thrusting a clenched fist at the old man's temple. He felt a crack as the man buckled and fell to the floor limply. Stepping over the body, he drew Idà Owurọ from its scabbard and raised his gaze towards the city.

To his left and right, a small distance away, the ends of two more rope ladders clacked against the rock, and the first of his unit landed softly on the rock behind him. Ahead was the 'shining jewel' of the Laruba Expanse: the city of Uzi. Its reputation was unearned, he felt. Its low, grass-covered buildings and knotted timber seemed unremarkable compared to the grandeur and scale of Obare and his Oorun Keep. At its centre was one large and uncharacteristically tall rotunda: Uzi Palace, the home of the Boy King. With focus unbroken, Agbaka marched forward. The rest would catch up. He glanced behind him; sharp shafts of light illuminated the final waves of soldiers descending the cliff face as the sun rose higher in the sky. In front of him on the other side of the valley, the Zufani were stationed. They had alternative plans for scaling the walls – long ropes shot from their siege machines to the floor below, along which specialists could slide. They were running behind by the look of things. No movement yet. No bother. Agbaka wasn't even sure he needed his army for this.

A throng of terrified peasants awaited him at the edge of their city, one sword, a burning torch and a thick metal chain between them. He twirled his great sword in his hand before charging in their direction. The sword-wielder heaved his weapon into the air and swung, wildly. Agbaka sidestepped, using the lateral momentum to arc Idà Owurọ through the man's torso. Blood cascaded across the floor to his right, prompting yelps from the three peasants who hadn't yet fled. Next came the man with the torch, himself supported by a boy who couldn't have seen more than 15 high-suns. In a display of bravery that almost stirred Agbaka, the boy charged forward with a knife; the man Agbaka assumed to be his father came too, the pair trying to flank him. Agbaka went straight for the boy, dropping his shoulder and thrusting his sword, to the hilt, into his gut. The boy careened backwards while Agbaka plunged forward into the older man, catching him in the chest. His eyes met Agbaka's as life faded from them. He angled his sword down and the body fell to the floor. The young boy had found his feet again, and even more courage. He screamed as he charged, knife first, towards Agbaka. Agbaka stood straight, took a breath and swung. The boy's head rolled from his shoulders; Agbaka stepped aside to let the momentum carry the body forward and past him to the floor. The man with the chain needed no further convincing. He fled, fast. Agbaka scanned the horizon to find the domed roof of the palace ahead.

Alone, he marched onwards, single-minded.

Sounds of fighting had begun to echo between the walls of the valley. Shrieks from Uzians finally understanding their rightful place in this world; grunts and sword swipes from his own army, exerting theirs. Agbaka moved through the streets of Uzi with ease. His blood-spattered body and gleaming great sword were enough to put off most from approaching. A full-throated growl was enough to put off the rest. Anyone who did attack was met with a swift demise.

The palace was better guarded – the closest thing Uzi had to a military presence was the palace's Ibhotwe Guard. There were four of them stood, spears in hand, at the palace gate. Finally, he thought, a challenge. Their spears lowered as their eyes met his. The fear was better masked among these men.

'HOLD!' one called.

Agbaka's pace quickened to a run. Gripping the dawn sword tightly in his hands, he plotted his foot placement in a blink of an eye. In the space of a breath, they were dead; with no more than a slice across his upper left arm, and even that felt good.

He kicked his way through the palace gates to find an empty courtyard. That didn't make sense. Where were the rest of the guards? He powered forward, through the door. A large hall awaited, resplendent with silks hanging from the ceiling, jewelled metalwork fastening the inner timber together with garish excess. And not a single person. He grunted in frustration and headed for the ladder at the far end of the room. Hiding in his bed-chamber, was he?

There was nothing there either. The whole palace was empty. Agbaka found his way over to the front of the building and out onto the balcony above the courtyard. From there, he could see the battle unfolding in the city below and the vast shimmering sea beyond that. His army had well and truly arrived and was pouring into the city from the northwest. The Zufani were still motionless atop their side. A logistics issue, surely. They knew better than to betray him. He could make out the cliff foot, a little further south. His advance team had opened the gates to the pass above, where the Obare Lancers had been lining up, now streaming through. That was when he spotted him. Up at the top of that same pass and coming in fast – a boy in a deep blue cloak astride a brown horse. Xola, The Boy King.

He was completely alone. The horse began charging down the valley towards the most fearsome battalion of warriors this world had ever known. Why? He panicked for a moment. What if Soasoro didn't recognise the boy charging forward? The Boy King was to be Agbaka's kill. He spotted something else: a giant, black bird had taken off from behind Xola. It was difficult to make out at first, but as it rose higher in the sky, it became impossible to ignore and just as impossible to comprehend. Like the stars at dawn, objects in the sky were snuffed out one by one by an advancing darkness. Agbaka watched on, astonished, as clouds and birds vanished, and the horizon to the north was wiped out. This was no dusk though: no purple hues or deep blue to follow, no shimmer of moonlight nor twinkling stars – and the sun still rose. But then it was gone too. By the time Agbaka had made it out of the palace, the darkness had spread above him. He got one last glimpse of his hands before him before the great night eagle plunged him into an unbroken darkness. His heartbeat quickened. He could see nothing. He reached around with his hands and, sure enough, he was still there – his body, his legs, Idà Owurọ, the ground beneath him: all still there. But all he could see was a deathly and unshakable blackness. He was blind.

★★★

Asi's pace quickened as the undergrowth that carpeted the forest floor began to thin and the shafts of dawn light became more plentiful than shadow. Amira clung tightly to Xola's torso. It had no doubt been some time since she'd ridden a horse. It was the first time he'd ridden one into battle. The sword she'd given him, a relic of his ancestors, hung heavy on his hip.

He had no idea what awaited him when he cleared the treeline. He winced at every blast of sunlight, fearful they'd left it too late. What if all that lay ahead was rubble? Even the Black Equinox couldn't save the dead.

It wasn't long before they were fully bathed in light. The sun sat low on the horizon to the east, forcing Xola into a squint. He could just about make out the precipice of Uzi valley ahead. Asi's eyes were better and she skidded to a stop, just short of the edge. He braced himself for the sight.

It was chaos. The first thing he noticed was the fire: entire portions of his city were ablaze. His arms began to tremble, but not with fear. Something else. He watched as legions of Obare swordsmen poured into the city from the ends of rope ladders suspended from nets fixed high up on the cliffs to his left. Ahead, on the valley's far cliff, he could make out the Zufani encampment, unmoved from their positions. At least the attackers were not yet in full force. He felt Amira shift in the saddle behind him, peering over his shoulder to the scene below.

'Whatever happens next, Xola… remember you had no choice.'

'And what happens next?' He regretted the question immediately. He wasn't ready to hear the answer.

She whispered.

'Lands with lakes and bountiful rivers were created for man to live. And the wide deserts so that he can find his soul. May the stars guide you, King Xola.'

Xola kicked Asi into action. She burst forward towards the top of the valley pass. The trembling had moved from his arms to his shoulders and down his spine where it became a rumbling within him. The thought of all this pain and anguish being wrought upon his people drowned out all other thoughts and the feeling it created within him was like nothing he'd ever known. It was as though the blood pumping through his veins had doubled in volume, looking to force its way through his skin, take control of his body and use him for its own ends. The sounds of the battle below seemed to ebb and flow in his ears; the shouts of anguish, thumping of war drums and clashes of steel cascaded across his attention like waves before crashing over him and swallowing him up, reducing this soundscape to a muffled rumble. It joined the one within him until that's all there was. Even his sense of self seemed to vanish. For a moment, there was no Xola, no Khanyishiwa, no Uzi, no Obare. There was only fury.

As he rounded the corner, Xola felt Amira evaporate and watched as her twinkling light scattered itself over his arms, casting his mounted silhouette in a long foreboding column ahead. She took to the air and he watched as her shadow climbed above his own. At first, it was just that of an eagle, but before long the shape grew until it was not just the shadow of her winged form, but a wall of darkness.

Xola looked ahead, down the mountain pass. The gates were wide open, and beyond he could make out Obare's mounted division, the Obare Lancers, the most feared warriors in the Expanse. He gripped the hilt of his sword and pulled it from its scabbard. It felt comfortable in his hand, an extension of himself and one he could use to disgorge this unrestrainable sensation within him. He relaxed his body to accommodate the motion of Asi's ever-increasing pace as she charged down the pass towards this mass of elite warriors.

Asi moved quickly, but the Black Equinox moved faster. It wasn't long before Xola felt her sheet of darkness envelop him. For a moment, he could see nothing at all. But then his eyes adjusted. There was light. Amira's light. A silvery, star-like glow beamed down from her soaring body and cast an otherworldly shimmer across the rocky pass. All colour was gone, but it was not necessary. The edges of objects stood out in the darkness, picked out by her ghostly gleam. If Asi was affected by

Amira's sorcery, she didn't show it. She continued to barrel down the steep incline, picking her way through the rocky path with perfect precision. Xola looked down to see his sword, especially reflective in this star-lit night, and then ahead to the legion of spearmen at the foot of the cliff. Clearly, Amira's powers had reached them; their previously impeccable order had broken and gaps appeared in their ranks. Shouts of confusion rang out as they sought to anchor themselves in the darkness.

Asi needed no direction. Xola closed his eyes and took a breath. He let the fury flow through his body before returning his eyes to his target.

He braced, ready for whatever happened next.

The Black Equinox

Agbaka's breathing quickened. He could hear it. He could hear everything. Although the sound of the battle had shifted. The clashes of swords had diminished, replaced with cries of confusion across the battlefield. He wasn't the only one lost in that darkness. A strange feeling erupted within him, a hollowness in his chest that grew so wide that his soul had nowhere to go but into it. It was unfamiliar but unmistakable. This was fear.

He tried hard to calm his mind and to visualise where he was. With his left arm outstretched and his right clutching his sword, he worked his way forward. Eventually, and sooner than he'd expected, he met with the palace courtyard's outer wall. He turned to place his back against it, grateful for the small sense of security it offered. He worked his way in the direction of the gate, or so he assumed – it didn't come. He must have made a complete circuit before it gave way to the doors he'd burst through earlier. Carefully, and quietly, he felt his way through the threshold and into the thoroughfare, making sure to keep the wall to his back.

The sounds of fighting had picked up again, but they painted a different picture. This was no longer clashes of steel, but slaughter. Uzians barked orders to each other. Could they still see? There was nothing but cries of fear from his own men. Then he heard footsteps to his right. Slow and considered.

Someone advancing on him. He held Idà Owurọ out and adopted a fighting posture.

'Stay back, Uzian. I will kill you,' he blustered. The footsteps stopped. Agbaka swung the sword to and fro in front of him, advancing on his best guess of their position. The blade met nothing but air. The ground crunched behind him and he spun around, terrified.

'ENOUGH! FIGHT ME!' The thumping of his own heartbeat overwhelmed his senses, raging as it struggled to keep pace with the terror coursing through his body. He lunged forward, slashing down with fearsome force but only connecting with the earth. He heaved it out of the ground before a sharp searing pain shot up through his lower back. He instinctively reached to the wound, surprised to find the shaft of a spear buried in his lower torso. He swung once more in the direction of the spear-wielder – but again hit nothing. He turned and felt the end of the spear collide with the palace wall behind him. The explosion of pain was so immense that it brought him to his knees. He caught his breath and made up his mind. He let out a roar as he snapped the shaft of the wooden spear and ran as fast as his feet could carry him.

The fear was gathering momentum and showed no signs of abating. Agbaka wasn't sure where he'd run to but somehow felt safer in motion. He did his best to attune to the rest of his senses, hoping to find cues as to the layout ahead. They were unforthcoming. What he could sense was the air rushing over his face and body and the ground beneath him, which dampened occasionally, presumably blood pooling in the streets. The air was thick with smoke and the smell of fire but no temperature shift to say it was near. The beating of his own feet and desperate breaths swamped the soundscape, occasionally intercut with the sound of someone wailing in pain or crying their last in the near distance. It wasn't long before his feet met with the soft, wet flesh of a corpse and he was sent flying forward. He felt the taste of metal in his mouth as his head collided with a stone wall. He tried to find his feet, but the collision was too great; his internal sense of balance had vanished. He reached out his hands to steady himself but found nothing. He fell over again, landing on the corpse he'd just stumbled over. He rolled over and pulled it on top of him. Perhaps he would be safer dead. He tried to calm himself and slow his breath but peace wouldn't come. The fear of being found only made the ruse harder to maintain.

Agbaka lay like this for a moment, and all fight drained from his body. He shook as tears rolled from his eyes and carved paths through his blood-soaked cheeks. The sounds of battle had abated, but only slightly, and they seemed more distant. He worked hard to determine their direction but gave up, realising he had no sense of orientation at all. It didn't matter. Surely, the battle was lost. Just as stillness settled, he heard footsteps. He closed his useless eyes and prayed.

Xola, joining his men in battle with the Black Equinox

The Pig Paddock

By the time the darkness lifted, the sun had begun to set. Above the ocean, the night's brightest stars took their places in the deepening purple sky. The water was near motionless, a silver plane reflecting the scene of serenity above. At a glance, this vast expanse seemed untroubled by the horror just beyond its edge. In reality, even the mighty ocean was not beyond the reach of the hellscape on land. The Molili ran red and, subdivided by the delta, offloaded its atrocious cargo in all directions: a red fan of fear and fury. It was as though the land sought to exonerate itself of the day's events, to wipe the stain of suffering from its face. Of course, the earth was as responsible for the events in Uzi as the ocean was for the blood pouring into it. Xola felt no such absolution.

Xola could barely make sense of what he and his people had just done. *How did this happen?* It was not the sorcerous mechanics that deserted him; that had become clear by the time he'd silently carved his way through the tangle of lost lancers. When he reached his fellow defenders on the other side, ordered and alert, the scale of their advantage became brutally evident: they could see everything. Agbaka's army could not. The rest unfolded as surely as a river finds the ocean. And it was that fact that troubled him so: *how had the peace-loving people of this tranquil valley found themselves capable of such butchery, and with such ease? Had they been capable of it all along?*

As he made his way down the valley, he surveyed the battlefield, the once-beautiful city of Uzi. He did his best to smile and congratulate his compatriots on their 'victory', and distract them – and himself – from reality. But even the dim light of this portentous, wretched dusk did nothing to hide the dreadfulness. Nowhere in the city was free from death. Bodies, prostrate in motionless agony, carpeted the ground in their thousands. Their armour and weapons indicated they were mostly Obare, but Uzians were well represented too. The Zufani on the other hand had never moved from their cliff side, vantage and contributed nothing to this unfathomable scene. *Did they know the fate that awaited*

Agbaka? Or had they just bet on the right side?

He was on his way to the delta – a pig paddock specifically, one that sat just at the base of the valley. Uzi had no dungeons or jails. When someone broke the laws of their land, they'd be thrown in with the pigs for a night. Among all the commotion of the day's events, this solution seemed as suitable as ever. With the battle won, what to do with their single prisoner of war was the only outstanding issue for the King to attend to. As this torch lit patch of mud came into view, Xola was still no closer to a decision.

While the rumbling that guided and carried Xola through the false night had waned, a small fire remained lit for the one who'd broken their sacred peace. He felt it trying to ignite and animate him once more, but he worked hard to douse it and find calm. The Black Equinox's darkness had lifted; the time for violence was over. Or so he kept telling himself.

He greeted the Ibhotwe captain that kept watch, before making his way to the fence surrounding this makeshift prison. Just to his right sat the mighty Agbaka. He made a sorry sight. His utilitarian military garb had been reduced to rags. He sat, chained to a stake in the ground, hunched over and covered in a thick crust of mud and dried blood. At a quick glance, Xola may well have mistaken him for a pig. He remained completely still, eyes fixed on the ground, even as Xola climbed over the fence.

'Are you satisfied, Agbaka?'

Agbaka said nothing. Xola felt his face tighten and his breathing quicken. He felt a pang of indignation but dismissed it as unbecoming.

'Your army lies shattered and bleeding on the land of Uzi Valley. Do you have nothing to say for yourself?' He was more forceful that time, as though the fire within inhabited his words. It had the strange effect of emboldening him further. He stood taller and broader and relaxed in this newfound sense of security.

'I don't remember you being so quiet. Don't they call you 'The Dauntless'?'

Still, the prisoner gave him nothing. Xola wouldn't have it.

He drew his sword and placed it under Agbaka's chin. 'Look at me, *coward.*'

That one landed. Agbaka's body twitched and he let go a muffled grunt. Xola watched as his prisoner's face, a patchwork of blood and mud, lifted slowly. His eyes followed the silver blade to its hilt. Xola's hand gripped it tightly, quivering with restraint. Eventually, Agbaka's eyes flicked up and met Xola's gaze. His lips were tight and his eyes stiff in their glare. Amira's darkness had clearly lifted for him too. Xola felt a quick pang of nervousness, an echo of the fear this man used to inspire. But it passed quickly as his body caught up with his present. He hadn't noticed it until now, but for the first time since his visit to the Oorun Keep, Xola was not afraid.

'Do it. Boy King. Kill me.' Agbaka's voice was different too: quiet and hollow. And there was no malice in it either. The challenge was sincere. It was certainly on Xola's list of options, but something stayed his hand. Was it pity? He held Agbaka's gaze.

'And release you from your shame? You really are a coward.'

'I feel no shame, boy. I lost, but not on my terms.'

'Your terms were met, Agbaka. I heeded every last one of those demands. And still, you came.'

Agbaka let out a curdled chuckle. 'So kill me.'

It wouldn't take much: a shift of his weight, the extension of his arm and the world would be rid of its murderous emperor. But without the cover of the Black Equinox's darkness, it felt that much more real. This one would truly be no one's responsibility but Xola's.

But then he would be the one who killed Agbaka, the Dauntless. *What was one more death?*

Fearlessness And Failure

The blade's point scraped across caked mud as it shuddered under Agbaka's chin. Xola stepped forward and it slipped to meet the flesh where jaw met neck.

The boy was one sharp movement from ending Agbaka's life, and Agbaka was ready for it.

It wasn't fear that prompted this readiness. The fear had faded. And it wasn't cowardice either. He did not want to die. But he knew he should. All his work, everything he'd spent his life trying to achieve had come to this: failure. What use was the death of his father if all that came next was ruin? If Agbaka couldn't fulfil his one purpose on this planet, then what use was he? He also remembered Ojebun's words. Everything he had predicted had so far come true. His army was shattered and the survivors scattered to the wind. The only outstanding detail was Agbaka's head on a spike.

But, save for his unsteady hand, the boy did not move, and his glare remained unbroken. Agbaka could not read him. This was not the snivelling child he'd hosted in the Hall of Fallen Kings. He stood tall and assured, proud and angry. Quite what had shifted since their last meeting, Agbaka could not tell. He imagined it had something to do with the scores of lives the boy had ended today. A part of him almost felt proud. Maybe he had achieved something after all.

'What are you waiting for?'

Xola's gaze never faltered. Agbaka felt the tip of his sword break the surface of his skin as the tension within the boy tightened. He was ready. Agbaka closed his eyes. He felt a tear roll down his cheek.

'*I am sorry, father,*' he muttered softly to himself. The sword dropped. Xola softened.

'I'm not going to kill you, Agbaka.' He opened his eyes. 'You are an awful man. This world would be better if you'd never entered it. But you did. And here you are, at my mercy.'

Agbaka's head fell. He was angry at himself, at the weakness he'd shown. He let it replace his self-pity. He was to live, then.

'Why?' he asked.

'I'm going to let you go. You can return to your home and live out the rest of your days. But you will remember what happened here. And your people will remember too. I want that memory alive in as many people as possible. I want no one to forget what happened here.' Every word twisted in Agbaka's mind, stoking a dormant fury. 'You will never attack again. Uzi's peace is sacred. All peace is sacred.'

'I thought you'd have grown out of this naivety by now, boy. You're a hot-blooded killer. I can see it! Look at you!' he laughed.

'I did what I had to do. I'm nothing like you.' 'You are more like me than you know, boy.'

Agbaka felt for the binds behind him to see if they might loosen. They were tight, but not unbreakable. He didn't imagine this stake would take too much shifting either.

'Why, because I've killed people?'

'There is violence in all of us, Xola. The real difference between you and me is that I've always known that. War is inevitable. You'd do yourself and your kingdom service in remembering that.'

Xola's face twitched in search of a riposte. But none came. Instead, a heavy silence hung between them. Perhaps, even an understanding. For a moment, Agbaka's urge to murder this boy dissipated. Perhaps, he should accept his defeat gracefully and walk away.

Or maybe he should rip the stake out of the ground and beat the boy to death with it. Then, with unbound hands, fight off the lacklustre Ibhotwe guard and make for the plains above. That would feel better.

But what then? Make the long journey back to Obare with a spear wound in his back? There was no guarantee he'd survive. He remembered Ojebun's words of warning and the wild animals that may stalk his trek.

Xola knelt down and undid the bindings at his back, and cut the rope around his feet with his sword. He was completely fearless as he did so.

'We have an accord, then?' he asked as he stepped back. Agbaka winced as he stood; the pain in his back was profound. 'Yes, King Xola. We have an accord,' he said, with more than a hint of malice. He meant it though. He would not return to Uzi with an army. That lesson had been learned.

But there were other ways of dispatching a king. Quietly.

Peace unbroken. He'd done it before, after all. 'We'll meet again,' he said.

Xola, battle-ready

Damage

The stench of death had shown no signs of abating. Having been their last line of defence from the horrors of war, the walls of Uzi valley were now what kept them lingering. The dead had initially been buried in mass graves at the base of the valley, a liminal space between the city and the delta. But the shoreward breeze and intense heat from the sun put that plan to pasture. They quickly decided to break tradition and burn the bodies in enormous pyres by the ocean. The smell was less rancid but no less distinctive. For the fourth day in a row, the sun set behind the pyre's enormous column of smoke, casting Uzi valley in its shadow. For the fourth day in a row, Xola watched from his balcony, dutifully.

His own recovery had been quicker than he'd expected. He'd come away with nothing more than a few cuts and grazes; scars he wore proudly now. He had been quieter; he knew that even without his mother and Khanyishiwa insisting on pointing it out. They kept asking '*Why?*' and 'What troubles you so?' But it wasn't like that. He couldn't explain it really, he just found he had less to say. Khanyishiwa had been so worried about him that she offered moving into the palace to support him but this would be a taboo. Any woman who moves into the palace to be with Xola has to be his wife. No matter how much he loved her and cared about her, he looked deeply into her eyes and smiled as he gently told her not to worry, he will be okay. He was grateful for the company but found her incessant concern stifling. He was fine. In fact, he felt great. He felt powerful. He was no longer the scared little boy who trembled before Agbaka, the Dauntless. He had successfully defended his people from the greatest army this world had ever known. He had answered the call. He was a warrior. A king. Perhaps kings were just… quieter.

As night fell, he said a prayer for the fallen and returned to his bedchamber.

Sleep was still hard-won for Xola. The anger he'd discovered in battle rumbled on within him. It was quieter now and far from the all-consuming animator it had been, but it still wanted a role in how he governed his life – and sleep was not on its agenda.

Eventually though, after the final lights outside had been snuffed out, Xola drifted from the waking world and into a fitful slumber.

He was standing in the pig paddock, shivering in a cold wind. Ahead, picked out by shimmering starlight, was an armed figure, panting and poised. It was difficult to make out the features of their face. Agbaka? Urughu? Xola grasped at his hip for his sword, but there was none. Terrified, he ran until he couldn't anymore. There was no one behind him. He'd vanished between the trees. He felt his heart beating faster and the rumbling worked its way across the top of his shoulders. He looked up just in time; the figure leapt from the afrormosia tree he'd been cowering next to, sword first. Xola dived, barely avoiding the blade. He cleared the treeline almost instantly, and the soft ground gave way to cold sandstone. The gnawing inside him warned that the danger had not gone. He'd hide.

He made a quick dash for the Hall of Fallen Kings. It was pitch black in here. Amira's light could not reach this place. He felt for a sword and plucked it from its fastening. When the figure finally arrived, he was quick to react. It worked. The sword went straight through the figure's torso. The darkness lifted and left Xola bathed in firelight. The figure slipped off his weapon and fell to the floor. It was Agbaka's giant golden great sword in his hand, but the face was Yeye kaMpande's, shrivelled and twisted. Xola removed the head and hung it in its place next to Agbaka's, which sat on a spike. The sweet smell of rotting meat. He rode out, down the mountain pass and along the Molili. Asi knew the way. Night had fallen by the time he arrived at the smouldering ashes of Uzi. This was Agbaka's fault, so he went straight for the pig paddock. Up ahead, there was a figure shivering in the cold wind. He drew the great sword and let fury do the rest. Xola woke with a start, sweating and incensed.

Uzi looked awful. Peace truly had begotten prosperity; without it, she withered. He would see his city return to glory once more. He'd build it himself if he had to. But with what? They had nothing left.

Agbaka had made sure of that.

But what if he could get back what had been taken from them? Agbaka had not kept his word, the contract was surely void. Although, Xola didn't imagine the Emperor would be in much of a mood to return it. With the scale of his failure obvious, that tribute was his only success. He wouldn't give up without a fight. What if that was a fight Uzi could win? Obare's army was nothing but ash in the air, and their allies were in no rush to support him – the Zufani had made that clear. Xola had no army either, but one needn't look far for enemies of Obare. He could raise one and pay Agbaka a visit.

They'd return to Uzi what was rightfully theirs. It would be justice. It's what a king would do.

Xola, the young king

ABOUT THE AUTHOR

Daniel Epih is a writer from Nigeria who is on the verge of unveiling his debut fictional book to the world. Rooted in the vibrant tapestry of African culture and traditions, his writing reflects a deep connection to his heritage and a profound appreciation for the power of storytelling. Through the guidance and inspiration of his beloved grandfather, Daniel's storytelling journey began, ultimately leading him to pen his own narratives and share the essence of his people with the world.

Born and raised in what was once a great Empire nestled within the heart of Africa, Daniel grew up surrounded by rich oral traditions and captivating tales passed down through generations. From a tender age, he found himself enthralled by his grandfather's mesmerising storytelling sessions. In the evening hours, Daniel and his cousins and nephews would gather around the fire as their wise elders wove tales of their ancestors, mythical creatures, and great exploits. The stories transported young Daniel to a world teeming with magic, wisdom, and the values that defined their people.

These experiences left an indelible mark on his soul and laid the foundation for his future as a writer.

After years of dedication, Daniel is now ready to unveil his debut fictional book titled "The Black Equinox: Rise of Agbaka

In "Echoes of Tradition," Daniel weaves together a tapestry of interconnected tales, blending history, myth, and contemporary themes to create a multi-layered narrative. His words transport readers to the depths of Africa, offering glimpses into the lives of its people, their struggles, aspirations, and the timeless wisdom that shapes their existence.

ABOUT THE ILLUSTRATOR

Ashley Koa is a 16-year-old illustrator who has a passion for bringing stories to life through her art. She recently worked on illustrating "The Black Equinox: Rise of Agbaka" book and brought her unique style and creativity to the project. Ashley is known for her attention to detail and her ability to capture emotions and expressions in her drawings. You can connect with her on her Instagram account: @Kiwie.0w0.

www.ingramcontent.com/pod-product-compliance
Lightning Source LLC
Chambersburg PA
CBHW050728010526
44107CB00009B/772